Just getting started with FrameMaker?

MW01042624

Get free FrameMaker training

I've put together a quick course at techcomm.tools/free-fm-training to show you two things:

- Creating documents with FrameMaker will save you and your company money when you work efficiently
- You can easily learn the skills to edit content with unstructured FrameMaker in just a couple of hours

TC
2LS

Getting started with FrameMaker:

☑ Download 30-day trial
☑ Sign up for free training

techcomm.tools/free-fm-training

HTML5 Publishing training

I love finding out about who's reading my book, and the easiest way for me to get to know you is to bribe you with free stuff!

When you visit techcomm.tools/html5 and tell me who you are, you'll get 3 free lessons on HTML5 publishing with FrameMaker. The lessons are part of my larger Digital Publishing with FrameMaker course, but the lessons are more than just an intro into the topic. They give you what you need to produce default output and improve the branding of your digital project.

GET FREE HTML5 PUBLISHING TRAINING

Scan this code or visit techcomm.tools/html5 and I'll send you a 3-part video training series showing you how easy it is to get great online and mobile output from FrameMaker

Need something else?

Tech Comm Tools offers online courses, live classes, and help with specific problems too.

Visit techcommtools.com or see the final page of the book for details.

About the Author

Matt Sullivan is the founder of Tech Comm Tools. Along with FrameMaker training and consulting available at www.techcommtools.com, Matt helps organizations deliver content (including video and interactive media within their documentation) to online and mobile users.

Matt is an Adobe Tech Comm Partner, Adobe Certified Trainer, Adobe Certified Expert, and an Adobe Community Professional. He has produced (for Adobe) new feature videos for the past 5 versions of FrameMaker and the Adobe Technical Communication Suite.

He is the author of

- FrameMaker - Structured Authoring Workbook (2020 Release, this book)
- FrameMaker - Structured Authoring Workbook (2019 Release)
- FrameMaker - Structured Authoring Workbook (2017 Release)
- FrameMaker - Structured EDD Development Workbook (2020 Release)
- FrameMaker - Structured EDD Development Workbook (2019 Release)
- FrameMaker - Structured EDD Development Workbook (2017 Release)
- FrameMaker - Working with Content reference book (2017 Release)
- FrameMaker - Creating and Editing Content reference book (2015 Release)
- Publishing Fundamentals: Unstructured FrameMaker reference book (version 11)

You can find information about print and eBooks of these titles at www.techcommtools.com/books/

Both structured and standard (unstructured) courses are available at www.techcomm.tools/training-courses

Stay up-to-date with #techcomm content by signing up for his free newsletter at www.techcommtools.com/email-list/

Please connect with Matt (*mattrsullivan* on social platforms) and visit the Tech Comm Tools Facebook page at www.facebook.com/tc2ls/

When not working with clients, (and outside of soccer referee for Varsity high school, AYSO, and club matches) you'll find Matt surfing and playing beach volleyball with Marianne and his two daughters, or enjoying other things outside.

Reach Matt directly by emailing him at matt@techcommtools.com

FRAMEMAKER 2020 RELEASE, V16.0.1 STRUCTURED AUTHORING

*A workbook for self-paced
or instructor-led training*

Matt R. Sullivan

December 2020, Updated for
FrameMaker 2020 (v. 16.0.1)

Chapter 1: Organization of this workbook

Chapter 2: Documents

Chapter 3: Document Structure

Chapter 4: Editing Text

Chapter 5: Editing Structure

Chapter 6: Attributes

Chapter 7: Validation

Chapter 8: New Documents and Structure Shortcuts

Chapter 9: Cross-references and Footnote Elements

Chapter 12: Generating Books, Tables of Contents, and Indexes

Chapter 1: Organization of this workbook

This workbook assumes you are not yet familiar with FrameMaker. If you are already familiar with unstructured or structured FrameMaker, you may only want to briefly skim Chapter 1 and Chapter 2, as they explain what FrameMaker does (Chapter 1) and how you move around in the FrameMaker interface (Chapter 2).

Module Objectives

FrameMaker is a powerful and efficient tool for creating, writing, and distributing structured and unstructured documents which are then printed on paper, published to the Internet, or distributed online.

In this module, you will:

- Get familiar with FrameMaker capabilities and resources.
- Understand the purpose of FrameMaker.
- Identify the main features of FrameMaker.
- Get introduced to FrameMaker's primary tools for authoring structured documents.
- Gain a grasp of structured documents.

How to Think About FrameMaker

FrameMaker is a tool that helps you create technical content, and for purposes of this book, structured content. Structure models included with FrameMaker include DITA, S1000D, xDocBook, or custom XML/SGML models defined within your organization.

Depending on the structure model used, you might use FrameMaker to create books from chapter files, which have elements. Elements may contain text, objects, or other elements. Elements also may have associated attributes which further describe an element's characteristics and other descriptive information.

Formatting in a structured document is (primarily) separate from the content.

What Is XML?

Extensible Markup Language (XML) is an open standard for defining structure models that is in widespread use internationally.

XML-based content models can describe and create structured documents that are not dependent on any hardware, software, format, or operating system. XML-based content models let you create an enforceable content model that is portable and can be exchanged seamlessly with others who are set up to use that specific content model.

Why FrameMaker?

XML is an open markup language. FrameMaker manages the XML syntax for the author and provides a powerful graphical user interface which is easy to learn and use.

Using elements, the **Structure View** provides a view of the hierarchy of document structure. The **Element Catalog** guides the user easily through complex structures, and assists the user with valid element decisions at any location in the document. The **Validation** tool quickly locates invalid elements in the structure and assists the user in correcting invalid element errors.

FrameMaker Features

FrameMaker is a complete, structured publishing system that document developers can use to produce documents ranging from simple, single-page memos, to complex, structured, multiple-chapter books with imported graphics.

FrameMaker provides:

- An element hierarchy that organizes document content.
- Attributes that define element characteristics.
- A validation tool to assist with the correction of an invalid element structure.
- Full word-processing, editing, and edit-tracking capabilities.
- Flexible page design.
- Built-in graphics tools.
- Book building and revision management.
- Professional color control
- Stylized tables for organizing data and information.
- Conditional text for producing multiple versions of a document.
- Hypertext linking within a document and/or between documents.
- Templates for standardizing documents.
- Evaluation of mathematical equations.
- An online help system.

Word Processing Capabilities

FrameMaker includes a wide range of powerful features for creating complex documents, but FrameMaker can also be used to write a letter or prepare a simple flyer.

FrameMaker provides:

- Text-editing, including text drag-and-drop capability.
- Spell checking.
- Search capability.
- A thesaurus.
- Multiple file export outputs (PDF, SGML, HTML, HTML5, XML, etc.)
- Special characters
- Document, personal, and site dictionaries
- Equations

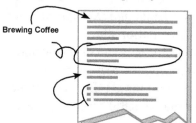

Special Copying Capabilities

Along with the standard *Copy* and *Paste* commands, there are commands to copy attribute values, paragraph formats, character formats, conditional text settings, or table column widths. These items can be copied to the Clipboard and pasted anywhere within the same document or within another document.

Text Formatting in Unstructured Content

 Formatting in structured documents is generally managed via the Element Catalog. See *FrameMaker - Structured EDD Development* at http://techcommtools.com/books/ for details.

Every FrameMaker document comes with a set of text formats, or styles. Relying on styles to change the format of text helps documents maintain a consistent, professional appearance.

- Paragraph Formats

  Paragraph formats determine how the titles, headings, lists, and text paragraphs appear on the page, including their font type, size, placement in table columns, spacing above and below text, autonumbering, tabs, and so on.

- Character Formats

  Character formats allows the application of many properties at the same time, as well as allowing you to change and add to the format characteristics of a text range within a paragraph. For example, a body paragraph may consist of plain text, but applying a character format to a text range can change the plain text to bold, overriding the original format. You might use this to bold glossary terms within a manual or use italics to emphasize a word or phrase.

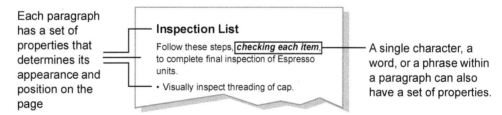

- Table Formats

  Table formats determine what a table looks like, text placement in the table columns (alignment, indentation, etc.), cell spacing, and so on.

Text Formatting in Structured Content

Because structured documents conform to a specific content model, FrameMaker can assign formatting rules to the content model itself, simplifying formatting efforts for structured content authors. The element catalog you will use in the exercises in this workbook formatting applied to the element definitions themselves.

Flexible Page Design

You can use FrameMaker in a number of ways to design pages in a document:

- Use FrameMaker XML templates.
- Use specially designed templates created by you, or someone else in your organization, to meet the day-to-day needs for simple documents, such as letters, or for more complex documents such as technical manuals.
- Create master (background) pages that contain the design elements you want to appear on any or all body (foreground) pages.

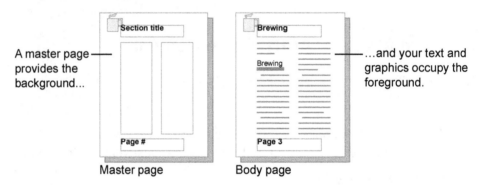

You specify the number and position of text columns and the appearance of background text and graphics.

Portrait (vertical orientation) and landscape (horizontal orientation) pages can be mixed and can contain any combination of columns.

Graphic Tools

To add visual appeal to a document, use FrameMaker drawing tools to draw and edit objects. Put graphics directly on the page, anchor the graphics to text, and prepare color separations for spot color and four-color process printing.

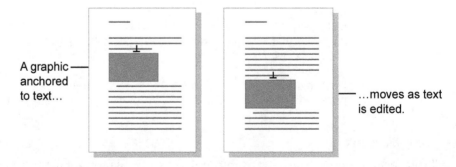

Book Building

FrameMaker provides a structured book-building feature that allows management of multiple files (chapters) to construct a single book. Create the book, add chapters, and then automatically generate a table of contents, list of figures, appendix, and index for the entire book.

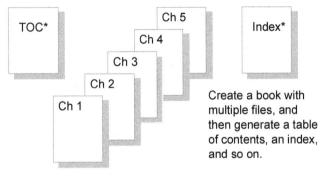

Create a book with multiple files, and then generate a table of contents, an index, and so on.

Revision Management

As you revise and refine a book, users can track changes by:

- Using *Track Text Edits*.
- Using change bars. Adding change bars marks changes made in the document with a vertical line in the margin.
- Comparing a current version of a document to an earlier version. A user can compare two documents to create a composite document and produce a summary document of all insertions, deletions, and changes.

Professional Color Control

FrameMaker provides different color systems or libraries for adding color to a document. A few are listed below:

- CMYK

  Different percentages of cyan, magenta, yellow, and black combine to create the color spectrum available in four-color process printing.

- PANTONE®

  Pantone colors are a commercially available library of custom colors.

- Online Color Library

  Provides 216 "web-safe" colors for online color consistency among all browsers

Users can review and correct color long before documents go to press, saving time and money.

Stylized Tables for Organizing Information

For presenting information in a tabular format, users can implement a FrameMaker table with any combination of lines and shading. Cells can be straddled to extend across several rows or columns. For a professional appearance, headings can be rotated to create table categories that stand out.

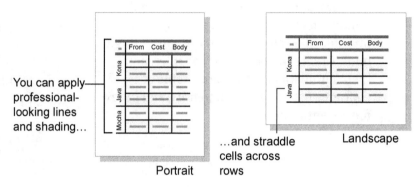

You can apply professional-looking lines and shading…

Portrait

…and straddle cells across rows

Landscape

Multiple Versions of a Document

FrameMaker conditional text and graphics allow a user to create and maintain one base document with multiple, convertible variations that can hide or display for printing.

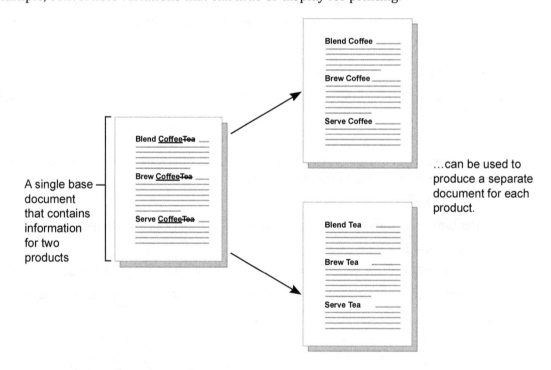

A single base document that contains information for two products

…can be used to produce a separate document for each product.

Use conditional text to produce separate documents for similar products, for example, or include hidden comments before sending the final copy to the printer.

Information Links

Use FrameMaker hypertext commands to set up links between locations in the same or different documents. Users viewing the document online need only click an active area to jump to related information.

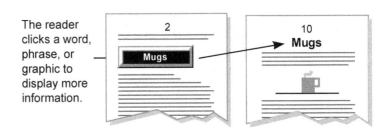

The reader clicks a word, phrase, or graphic to display more information.

Automatic Hypertext Links

When generating a Table of Contents (TOC) or Index for a manual, for example, a user can create hypertext links to the information in the source document simply by turning on a dialog box option. FrameMaker creates a clickable hypertext link from each entry in the generated file (e.g., TOC or index) to the page and location where the entry is located in the source document.

Templates for Standardized Documents

When creating a document from a structured template, the template's elements, attributes, page layouts, predefined formats, and other properties are used. Each document created from the template has a consistent look and can be easily updated when the design requires a change. FrameMaker comes with a variety of starter templates:

- Book (front matter, table of contents, chapter, and index)
- Blank paper
- Business card,\ and envelope
- FAQs
- Letter, memo, and fax cover
- Outlines
- Parts Catalog
- Reference Card
- Reports
- Structured templates for many of the above
- User Guide

Any template can be opened and the user can begin preparing a document. To better suit document requirements, a user can modify an existing template or create a template from scratch.

Typeset Mathematical Equations

FrameMaker provides a full palette of math elements to streamline the creation of typeset equations. Create an equation by inserting an equation object of a particular font size into a document, and then insert the math elements—numbers, symbols, operators, and so on—into the object.

After creating equations, a user can change their format—fonts, alignment, exact positioning of the math elements, and the amount of white space around them. There are even commands on the Equations palette to evaluate the equation mathematically.

Online Help System

FrameMaker's online help system (at **Help > Help Topics**) is a reference guide to FrameMaker commands and dialog boxes; the system explains what each command and dialog box does. If you can't find what you need via the bookmarks and starter topics, click in the Search bar to perform a full-text search on the system.

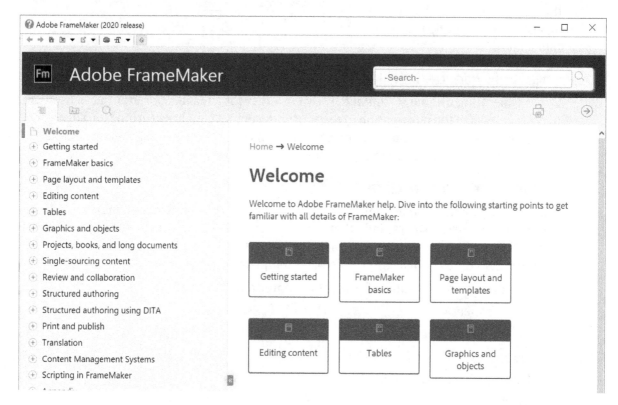

More About FrameMaker

When using FrameMaker, it may help to think of it as a page layout application. Everything viewable in a FrameMaker document window can be manipulated in a number of different ways. Objects can be cut, pasted, micro-positioned to within a thousandth of an inch, resized, moved from one document to another, and more.

But unlike other page layout applications like InDesign, FrameMaker is designed for predictable layout, rather than wholly customizable pages. FrameMaker's strength is in its rigidity and ability to provide consistency in formatting and pagination.

Structured FrameMaker in particular has set rules and options. When working in structured content you will not often customize formatting. Rather, you focus on the content and allow the formatting to be determined independently based on the structure of the document, whether the content will render on your editing screen, a PDF, or a mobile phone/tablet.

Graphic and Text Objects

There are two main classes of objects in FrameMaker—graphic objects and objects that contain text.

Graphic Objects

You can create quite complex diagrams and illustrations using FrameMaker's drawing tools. FrameMaker treats your created graphic objects, screen captures, and imported graphics in a variety of formats in the same way. For example, the rectangle at the top of the first page in this chapter is a graphic object.

Graphic objects have editable properties, such as size, position on the page, border width and pattern, fill pattern, and rotation. Objects can be moved on the page and positioned manually, or very precise controls can be used to very accurately position the objects.

Text Frames

There are two kinds of text objects in FrameMaker—text frames and text lines. Both types of objects will be wrapped in container elements that you will learn to place in future lessons. Much of your work in FrameMaker will be done in text frames. On the screen, text frames appear as dotted lines when using the **View>Borders** option. Pressing the **Enter** (return) key at the end of a line is not necessary, because text automatically wraps within a text frame. Text frames contain the elements and attributes inserted when authoring a structured document.

Text Lines

Text lines are simple lines of text. They do not wrap at the right margin. In fact, they have no margins whatsoever. They cannot contain tables or footnotes. If the **Enter** key is pressed, another text line displays.

On the other hand, you can select, group, align, and distribute text lines on the page. This makes a text line perfect for callouts or labels to use with diagrams and screen captures. When used in this way, text lines are considered parts of a graphic.

Layout

Using master pages, text and graphic objects can be manipulated to create both simple and complex layouts. Master pages can then be applied as needed to pages in the document. Master pages allow running headers and footers, page numbers, graphic elements, and text columns to appear consistently in the same place within chapter, index, and appendix pages.

Documentation Set

Whether a publishing novice or production expert, FrameMaker documentation software provides a clear and easy path to productivity. FrameMaker comes with a set of online and printed manuals at https://helpx.adobe.com/framemaker/help/help-resources.html.

Online Manuals

You can access the online help system by selecting **Help > Help Topics** from the main menu, or by selecting the Help toolbar icon (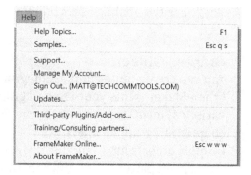).

Chapter 2: Documents

Introduction

In this module, you will become familiar with the basic features of FrameMaker. You will open a FrameMaker document, explore the document window, change your view of the document, save, and print it.

Module Objectives

In this module, you will learn how to:

- Start FrameMaker.
- Open, print, close, and delete documents.
- Use the *Save* and *Save As* commands.
- Set backup and save preferences.
- Tour the document window.
- Use zoom options.
- Use the *View* menu commands.
- Page through documents.

Starting FrameMaker and Opening a Sample File

 Don't yet have a license for FrameMaker 2020? You can download a free 30-day trial of FrameMaker at https://www.adobe.com/products/framemaker/download-trial/try.html

 Exercise 1:   Getting started
In this exercise, you will start the FrameMaker application.
If you are not sure how to start FrameMaker, do the following:

1. Press the **Windows** button (⊞), then start typing **FrameMaker** until you see the appropriate version of FrameMaker display in the **Search** window.
2. Click on the application icon to start FrameMaker.

If available, you can also double-click a FrameMaker icon on the desktop screen or one that is pinned to the task bar.

After startup, the FrameMaker welcome screen displays.

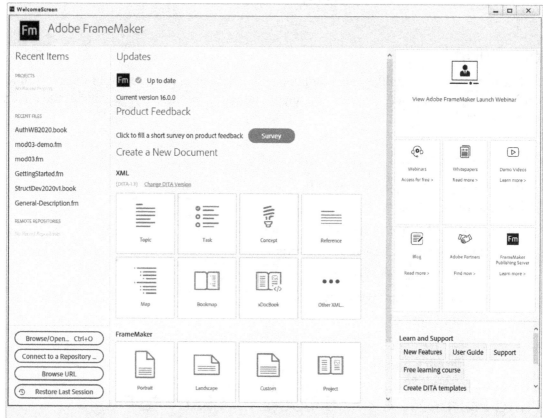

⋮☰ Exercise 2:   Opening a sample file

FrameMaker includes a number of templates and sample files from which you can create documents. In this exercise, you will open a sample unstructured file.

1. Select **Help > Samples** in the **Help** menu.

   The `Samples` directory window displays.

2. Double-click on the **UserGuide(Arabic, English, Hebrew)** directory folder.

   The `Arabic`, `English`, and `Hebrew` directory folders display.

3. Double-click on the **English** directory folder.
   The `Personal Spaceship User Guide` files and folders display.

4. Double-click on the **General-Description.fm** file.

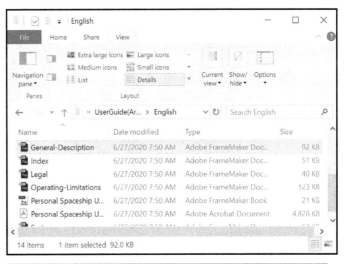

5. An alert may display.
Click the **OK** button to convert the file to the current version of FrameMaker.

The `General-Description.fm` file opens.

Menu Bar —

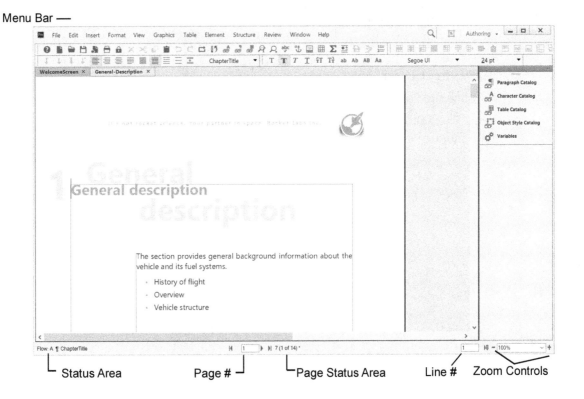

Saving Documents

The `Samples` directory is in a protected location, so the easiest way to save changes to files opened from the `Samples` directory, is to save it to another location.
To do this, you use the **Save As** command.

 Running FrameMaker in Administrator Mode will, among other things, allow you to save changes to the `Samples` directory. For details on how to run FrameMaker as Administrator, see a sample video from my FrameMaker course at https://vimeo.com/mattrsullivan/review/228437644/aa2af50c43.

Exercise 3:   Using Save As

In this exercise, you will rename and save a file using the **Save As** command.

1. Use the **Save Document** dialog box to save the document in a writable directory with the new filename `General-Description1.fm`.

   a. Select **File > Save As** from the main menu.

      The **Save Document** dialog box displays.

   b. Double-click on or navigate to the `Desktop` directory folder, if necessary.

   c. In the **File name** field, change the filename to `General-Description1.fm`

   d. Click the **Save** button.

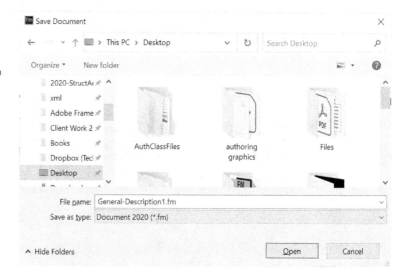

2. Select **File > Close** from the main menu.

Exercise 4:   Opening a file and using the Save command

The **Save** command is used to save changes to an existing document. The table below describes when to use the **Save** command, rather than the **Save As** command.

Use:	If:
Save	The document has been saved before and you want to use the same directory, filename, and permissions to save the document in a standard FrameMaker format.
Save As	Use this option if you want to change the directory, filename, or permissions for the file. In addition, if you're saving a document in a format other than the normal FrameMaker format, you need to use *Save As*.

1. From the `Class` directory, open the `General-Description1.fm` document saved in the previous exercise.

    a. Select **File > Open** from the main menu.

    The **Open** dialog box displays.

    b. Navigate to the `Desktop` directory.

    c. Double-click on `General-Description1.fm` to open the file.

    The file you saved in the previous exercise displays.

 A quick way to open a recently opened file is to select **File > Open Recent** from the main menu and selecting the file name from the list.

2. Near the top of the first paragraph of text, click just before the word "vehicle".

3. Make a simple change to the document by dragging the mouse to highlight "vehicle", and type in the word `rocket`.

4. Select **File > Save** from the main menu.

The section provides general background infc vehicle and its fuel systems.

  * History of flight

Automatically Saving and Backing Up

A FrameMaker document can be saved three different ways:

* Use **Save** or **Save As** commands to manually save a document.

* Set your preference for Automatic Backup on Save. This feature automatically make a backup of the existing file *before* you manually save changes. With this feature enabled, even if your system crashes while saving (or a file otherwise becomes unusable) you will have the previously saved version available on disk.

* Set your preference (**Edit > Preferences**) to use the Auto Save feature. This doesn't automatically save your working file to disk, but instead creates an .autosave file in your working directory. By enabling this feature, if you experience a power failure or other system crash you will have a working file saved to your disk with minimal lost work.

See the following exercise for a screenshot of the Preferences dialog.

Recovering After a Crash

FrameMaker keeps a log of your most recent changes. In the event of a system or FrameMaker crash, FrameMaker writes this log to a Recovery file (.recover). After a system crash, you can usually start working from the recover file without losing any of your work.

Summary of File Names

Here are the file extensions used by various backup file formats:

Autosave Files	**Backup Files**	**Recover Files**
{filename}.auto	{filename}.backup	{filename}.recover

 ## Exercise 5:   Setting backup and save preferences

In this exercise, you will set backup and save preferences. These settings will affect all open files while FrameMaker is running.

1. Select **Edit > Preferences** from the main menu. The **Preferences** dialog box displays.

   Your current settings may differ from those shown.

   The **Preferences** dialog manage controls and operations for the entire editing session, not just for an individual file.

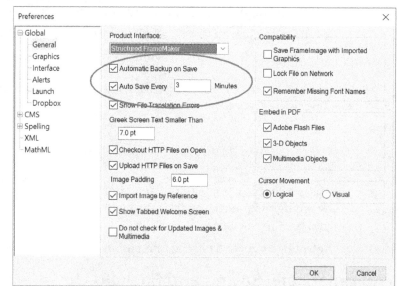

2. Select (turn on) **Automatic Backup on Save** (if not on already) by clicking in the check box.

3. Select (turn on) **Auto Save Every _ Minutes** (if not on already) by clicking in the check box.

4. Change the **Auto Save** minutes interval to **10** minutes.

   a. Double-click to select (highlight) the number in the **Minutes** field, if applicable.

   b. Type: `10`

   c. Click **OK** button and restart FrameMaker.

      Now, as you work on `General-Description1.fm`, FrameMaker will write the most current contents to an autosave file every 10 minutes.

Whenever you use select **Save** or **Save As**, the autosave file is deleted and the autosave process starts over again at the specified 10-minute interval. This autosave process occurs not only for `General-Description1.fm`, but for all other currently open documents as well.

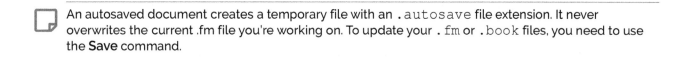

An autosaved document creates a temporary file with an `.autosave` file extension. It never overwrites the current .fm file you're working on. To update your `.fm` or `.book` files, you need to use the **Save** command.

Controlling Document Zoom

Zoom options allow you to:

- Magnify text and objects (zooming in, making the display larger).
- Make text and objects appear smaller to fit more in the window (zooming out, making the display smaller).

Exercise 6:   Zooming

In this exercise, you will change the zoom using some preset zoom settings.

1. In the status bar at the bottom right of the document window, click the **Increase Zoom** button (+) twice.

   The Zoom status now indicates that the document has been enlarged to 140% of its original size.

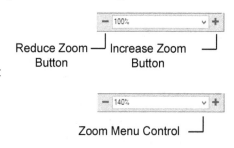

2. Select **View > Rulers** from the main menu.

   The rulers at the top and left of the document window show the actual size of the document, regardless of zoom.

   Once you begin working in structured documents, you won't use the rulers for anything so consider turning off display of rulers.

3. Click the **Zoom** menu button(⌄).

   The zooming size options display.

4. Move the pointer to **150%** and click the mouse button.

   The document enlarges to 150% of its original size.

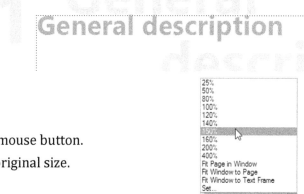

5. Click the **Reduce Zoom** button (![-]).

   The document reduces from 150% to 140% of its original size.

   Depending on the size of your FrameMaker window, the page may be cut off at the bottom and and right side of the document.

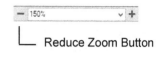
Reduce Zoom Button

> Since zoom settings are saved with the document, an asterisk (*) will appear in the status bar, next to the page count when a change has been made to the zoom settings.

6. Click the **Zoom** menu button and select **Fit Window to Page**.

   The document remains at 140% of its original size, but on wider monitors, the width of the document window increases so that the page is no longer cut off.

7. Click the **Zoom** menu button and select **Fit Window to Page**.

   The zoom percentage remains the same, but on larger monitors the width of the window decreases to match the width of the document.

Using View Menu Commands

FrameMaker provides a number of guides—borders, text symbols, rulers, grid lines, and element boundaries—to help you work with a document. You can turn them on and off while working in a document.

> Borders, text symbols, rulers, and grid lines do not print. However, Element Boundaries and Element Boundaries (as Tags) do print if turned on from the View menu.

Rulers

Rulers can be displayed at the top and left side of the document window. **Rulers** are useful for locating a position on a page and placing graphics.

Borders and text symbols

During the editing process, many authors prefer to have document text symbols and borders turned on. **Borders** help to identify the text areas on the page.

Symbol:	Meaning:
¶	End of paragraph
§	End of flow
❯	Tab

FrameMaker also provides two symbols to display element boundaries when working with structured documents. While you won't see them displayed in this unstructured document, these boundaries will be important tools that you will use for the remainder of this course.

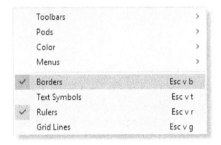

Symbol:	Meaning:
[ ]	Opening and closing Element Boundaries in the document window
−List / List	Opening and closing Element Boundaries as Tags in the document window

Exercise 7: Viewing borders, text symbols, and rulers

In this exercise, you will turn on various options and reset ruler increments and display units.

1. If not already visible, select **View > Borders** from the main menu to display dotted lines around text frames and other objects on the page.

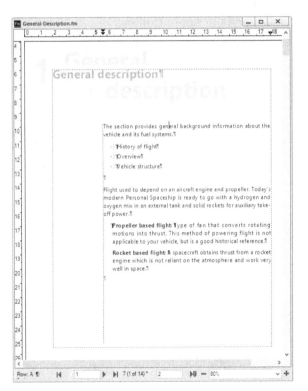

2. If not already visible, select **View > Text Symbols** from the main menu.

   Text symbols appear throughout the document.

3. If not already visible, select **View > Rulers** from the main menu.

   Rulers appear at the top and left edges of the document window. In the document above, rulers currently display in picas.

4. Select **View > Options** from the main menu.

   The **View Options** dialog box displays.

   Display Units may currently display **cm**, indicating that units in text boxes will be displayed in the centimeter measurement. For example, the **Grid Spacing** text box shows **0.2 cm**; not the equivalent in inches.

5. From the **Display Units** drop-down menu, select **Inch**.

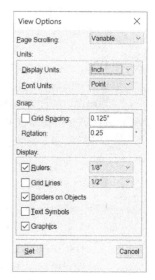

 You can use other units of measure (like **in** or **"** for inches, or **mm** for millimeters. You can also perform calculations inside most dialogs.

6. Click the **Set** button.

   Dialog boxes now will use inches as their default units of measurement, rather than centimeters.

7. Select **View > Options** from the main menu.

   Notice the **Grid Spacing** text box has changed to display inches, rather than centimeters.

8. Select **1/8"** from the **Rulers** drop-down menu.

9. Click the **Set** button.

   The ruler increments change to **1/8"**.

Changing Pages

There are many ways to move through a document; scrolling, the page buttons, the **Go To Page** buttons, and keyboard shortcuts. A table of the keyboard shortcuts is shown below.

 In the following keystroke combinations, a plus sign (+) means that two keys should be pressed simultaneously; a space indicates that keys are pressed in a sequence.

To Display	Press
Previous page	**Page Up** or **Esc p p**
Next page	**Page Down** or **Esc p n**
First page in document	**Alt + Page Up** or **Esc p f**
Last page in document	**Alt + Page Down** or **Esc p l**

Scrolling

To scroll through a document, use the scroll bar on the right side of the document window. The scroll bar is especially useful when you want to see an entire paragraph, a list, or other text that spans two pages.

 Exercise 8: Scrolling

In this exercise, you will use the scroll bar to move through the document.

1. Click the **down scroll arrow** and hold mouse button down until the document scrolls a few pages.

   The document scrolls down continuously.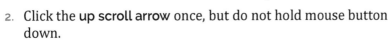

2. Click the **up scroll arrow** once, but do not hold mouse button down.

   The document moves up one line.

3. Click the **up scroll arrow** and hold mouse button down until the document scrolls back toward the top of document.

4. Locate the **scroll box** at the top right of the document window.

5. Drag the **scroll box** down to toward the bottom of the **scroll bar**.
   The document scrolls quickly toward the last page of the document.

6. Drag the **scroll box** back to the top of the **scroll bar**.
   You quickly land on the first page of the document.

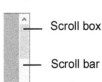

— Scroll box

— Scroll bar

Exercise 9:   Paging

In this exercise, you will use the page buttons to change pages. Page buttons are quick and easy to use when you want to go forward or backward in a document.

1. Click the **Go to Next Page** button (▸) in the status bar.

Go to Next Page button

Page **2** displays and **8 (2 of 14)** displays in the Page Status area.

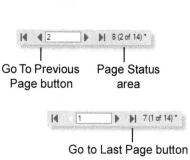

Go To Previous Page button   Page Status area

2. Click the **Go to Previous Page** button in the status bar. Page **1** displays and **7 (1 of 14)** displays in the Page Status area.

3. Click the **Go to Last Page** button (▸|) in the status bar to view the last page of the document.

Go to Last Page button

4. Click the **Go to First Page** button (|◂) in the status bar to return to the first page of the document.

Exercise 10: Using the Go To Page box

In this exercise, you will use the **Go To Page** dialog box to move to a particular page.

1. Click **View > Go to Page** from the main menu. The **Go to Page** dialog box displays.

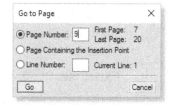

2. In the **Page Number** text box, type: 9

3. Click the **OK** button.

Page 3 displays in the **Page** field, and **9 (3 of 14)** displays in the Page Status area at the bottom of the document window.

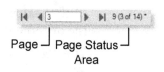

Page ⏊ Page Status ⏊ Area

4. Double-click to highlight the **3** in the **Page Number** field at the bottom of the document window, type: 2, and press **Enter**.

Page 2 displays in the Page field, and **8 (2 of 14)** displays in the Page Status area.

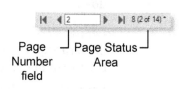

Page Number field   Page Status Area

5. Select **File > Save** from the main menu.

Printing Documents

You can customize printing options by changing settings in the **Print** box.

 Exercise 11: Printing

In this exercise, you will review the steps to print a document. You will cancel the print command after reviewing the print options.

1. Select **File > Print** from the main menu. The **Print Document** dialog box displays.

   Notice that you can specify the page range, number of copies, and other settings.

2. Click the **Cancel** button.

Recognizing changes made to a document

FrameMaker indicates that changes have been made to a document by placing an asterisk at the end of the **Page Status Area**. Before closing, you have the option to save or not save changes that you have made.

 Exercise 12: Closing and saving changes

In this exercise, you will close a document and save changes to it at the same time.

1. Click anywhere in the text of the document and make a type change.

   Notice that an asterisk (*) displays in the status bar at the bottom of the document window to indicate that a change has been made to the document.

Asterisk

2. Select **File > Close** from the main menu. The **Save File** dialog box displays and asks if you want to save the changes before closing.

3. Click the **Save** button.

   The document disappears from the screen, and changes are saved to the disk.

If you close out of FrameMaker with a series of documents open, the **Save Files** dialog may display. This convenient dialog allows you to quickly choose which (if any) files you wish to save prior to exiting the application.

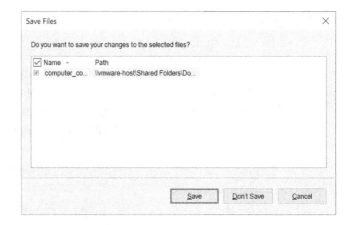

Optional Exercise

The following exercise enables you to enhance your FrameMaker skills and to explore additional features. The steps are intentionally brief and require more independent thought on your part.

 Exercise 13: Using shift commands

In this optional exercise, you will explore two "shift" commands you can use when you have several files open at the same time. Shift commands are alternate versions of FrameMaker commands that become available when you hold down the **Shift** key before accessing the menu on which the command appears.

1. Open `General-Description1.fm`, and make a change to the document, but do not save it.

2. Navigate to **Help > Samples > overview**, and open the `resume.fm` file.

3. Select **File > Save As**, and save `resume.fm` with any name you want into your `Class` directory.

4. Change the name **Chris Smith** on the resume to your name.

5. To save all open documents, press and hold the **Shift** key, and select **File > Save All Open Files**. The **Save All Open Files** command replaces the **Save** command on the File menu when the **Shift** key is pressed.

6. To close all open documents, press and hold the **Shift** key and select **File > Close All Open Files** from the main menu. The **Close All Open Files** command replaces the **Close** command on the File menu when the **Shift** key is pressed.

Chapter 3: Document Structure

Introduction

In this module, you'll become familiar with the FrameMaker structured editing environment.

Module Objectives

In this module, you'll learn how to:

- Download and access data files for exercises
- Open and manipulate elements in the **Structure View**.
- Position insertion points in **Structure View**.
- View **Element Boundaries** in the document window.
- View **Element Boundaries (as tags)** in the document window.
- Select elements in the document window and **Structure View**.
- Expand and collapse elements in **Structure View**.
- Use the keyboard to navigate through elements in **Structure View**.
- View attributes in **Structure View**.
- Open and manipulate the **Element Catalog** list.
- Create a customized **Element Catalog** list.
- Review a list of element terms.

Download Course Data Files

 Exercise 1:   Download and expand course data files

In this exercise, you will access the files needed to complete the rest of this course.

1. Ensure that your computer is connected to the internet.

2. Open a browser (Explorer, Chrome, Firefox)

3. Navigate to
   http://bit.ly/fm-auth-files
   in the browser.

   You'll be redirected to the page shown here:

4. Fill out the form to get the workbook files sent to you via email.

5. When prompted, save the **AuthClassFiles.zip** file to your computer.

6. Decompress the files using Windows or your favorite decompression utility.

 Files will not work properly unless decompressed.
Contact me at matt@techcommtools.com if you need assistance decompressing your files.

 The ZIP file provided contains workbook-specific files for each FrameMaker release since 2015. The exercises and dialogs shown in this workbook will not completely align if used with FrameMaker 2019 or earlier, and you may want to consider using the workbook for your specific version instead of this one.

FrameMaker Document Pages, Formatting, and Structure

Body pages, master pages, and reference pages

Authors spend most of their time in FrameMaker working in the *Body Pages* of a document. These are the printable pages where you insert *Elements*, enter and edit text (not including headers and footers), and create and/or import graphics.

Other types of pages are used to format the body pages in a consistent manner. *Master Pages* apply background objects, such as headers and footers, to document pages.

Reference Pages add objects to individual paragraphs. Reference pages also contain information needed to construct generated files, such as tables of contents and indexes.

Master Pages and Reference Pages are often managed by a template designer, an experienced user who understands formatting options. Master and Reference pages generally do not require modification by authors.

Occasionally, you may need to apply a specific master page to a body page in the document.

If you are the template designer, you may need to adjust master pages to adjust page layout information, such as running headers and footers, page numbers, and the size and location of text areas.

Text formatting

In an unstructured FrameMaker document, paragraphs are formatted using a variety of text styles. In a structured FrameMaker document, formatting is applied to elements based on rules in the **Element Catalog**, which apply text formatting such as font size and font weight, as elements are being inserted or changed, or content is wrapped. In some cases, formatting may change based on an element's context, or relationship to other elements.

 Modifying paragraph and character formats in a structured document is not advised.
Changes to these formats may cause unexpected results when saving to XML.

Structure characteristics

You build document structure by adding and arranging *Elements* to your document. These elements organize the contents of the document, such as its text, graphics, and tables.

The **Structure View** provides a hierarchical representation of the document's structure. It shows you the elements and their attributes. *Element boundaries* (when displayed) show you where the elements begin and end.

FrameMaker also provides two symbols (accessed from the **View** menu) to display element boundaries when working with structured documents. These boundaries are important tools that you will use for the remainder of this course:

Symbol:	Meaning:
[ ]	Opening and closing Element Boundaries in the document window
−List / List	Opening and closing Element Boundaries as Tags in the document window

- *Element Boundaries.* **Element boundaries** are square brackets surrounding each element in the document window. This option will be useful later in this course when you start inserting elements via the keyboard.

- *Element Boundaries (as Tags).* **Element boundaries (as Tags)** display the element's name surrounding each element in the document window.

 Exercise 2:   Viewing the structure

In this exercise, you will open a sample file, learn how to display the **Structure View**, and turn on **Element Boundaries** in the document window.

1. From the `AuthClassFiles2020` directory, open `Chapter03.fm`.

    a. Select **File > Open** from the main menu.

        The **Open** dialog box displays.

    b. Navigate to the `AuthClassFiles2020` directory you created in Exercise 1, if necessary.

    c. Double-click `Chapter03.fm`.

        The document displays in the document window.

2. If necessary, make borders visible by selecting **View > Borders**.

    Viewing borders can help navigate "live" areas where you can edit content within your document.

3. If necessary, turn off rulers and text symbols by deselecting those options in the **View** menu.

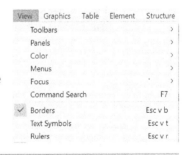

In this course you'll learn to focus attention on the **Structure View** when doing many activities. Turning off the **Text Symbols** and **Rulers** will help you learn to rely less on the **Document View**.

4. Place your cursor inside the title, **Data Communications**.

5. Select the **Structure>Structure View** menu item..

The **Structure View** displays.

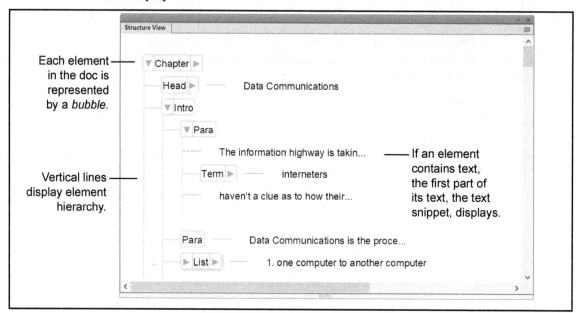

A round-cornered rectangle represents a container element which will contain text and/or other elements.

A square-cornered rectangle represents a FrameMaker object, such as a graphic, cross-reference, variable, or marker.

The triangles on the right expand and collapse elements containing additional structure. The triangles on the right expand and collapse attribute display. You'll learn about each of these things shortly.

6. Dock or expand the **Structure View** pane to the right side of your screen so that you can view both the **Structure View** pane and the document window.

7. Select **View > Element Boundaries (as Tags)** from the main menu. A set of arrow-shaped icons with an element name appear in the document window around each text element. The element boundaries can wrap a range of text, or can wrap one or more elements. Note how the tags match in both the document and structure view.

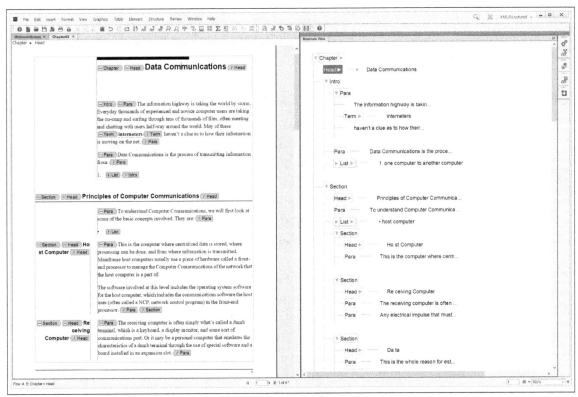

8. Select **View > Element Boundaries** from the main menu.

   The verbose tags are replaced with a set of brackets around each element in the document window. These brackets take up less space than the full tags.

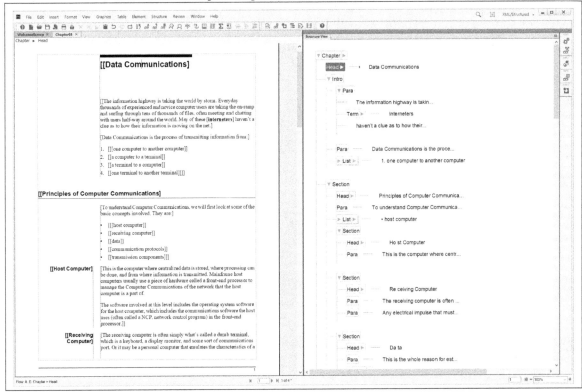

Viewing **Element Boundaries** or **Element Boundaries as Tags** is largely a personal preference. In this workbook you'll use the **Element Boundaries** option to remain concise and consistent.

Manipulating Elements

You can manipulate elements in both the document window and the **Structure View**. Elements can be moved, deleted, changed, inserted, cut, copied, and more.

Selecting elements

Elements can be selected in the document window or in the **Structure View**. In the document window, you select elements by dragging the mouse to highlight the text.

In the **Structure View**, you select an element by clicking on one of the element bubbles.

Parent, child, sibling, ancestor, and descendant relationships

Descendants in the **Structure View** are defined by the relationship between a parent element and its subordinate child elements, called descendants of the parent element. Elements on the same level of hierarchy are considered siblings of the same parent.

For example, a chapter element might have a child called Head, which contains the chapter's title. The chapter might also have another child called Section, which is a sibling of Head. Multiple section elements are considered siblings of each other.

A paragraph can also be a descendant (or child) of the section, due to its position in the hierarchy in the **Structure View**.

Similarly, you can follow the lines upward from elements to determine their ancestors.

For simplicity, in this book we will most often discuss the parent/child relationship.

These parent, child, and sibling element relationships determine where elements are located in the **Structure View** hierarchy.

Exercise 3:   Selecting elements in the Structure View

In this exercise, you will practice selecting elements in the **Structure View.**

1. Click the first **Head** element bubble under the **Chapter** element in the **Structure View.**

    The **Head** element in the **Structure View** and its text content in the document window are selected.

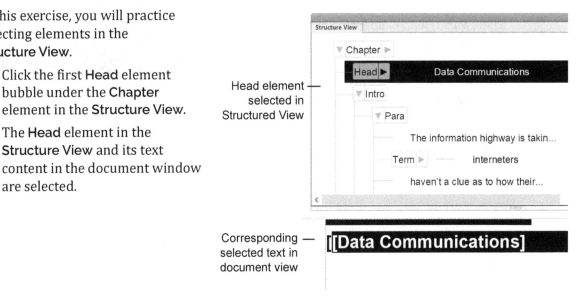

Head element selected in Structured View

Corresponding selected text in document view

2. Click the first **List** element bubble in the **Structure View.**

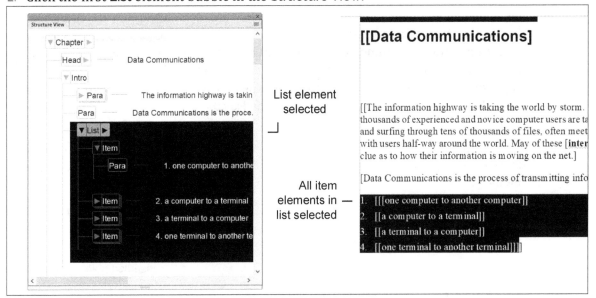

List element selected

All item elements in list selected

The **List** element and all of its descendants (children/siblings) are selected in the document window and the **Structure View.**

3. Select the **Chapter** element at the top of the **Structure View.**

    All elements in the document are now selected because **Chapter** is the document's highest-level element, and all other elements are contained within the **Chapter.**

4. Click on the **Head** element under the first **Section** element.

5. Press and hold the **Shift** key, and click the **Para** element below the **Head** element.

   Both the **Head** and **Para** elements are selected. If desired you would now be able to delete these elements or wrap them in additional structure.

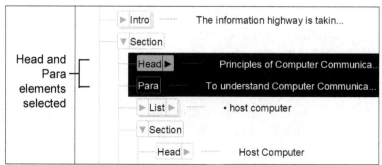

Exercise 4: Positioning the insertion point

In this exercise, you will practice positioning the insertion point and identify your location within the structure hierarchy.

1. Place your insertion point as shown between the **Chapter** and **Head** elements in the **Structure** View.

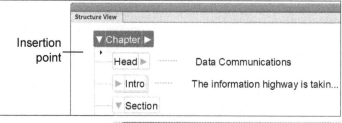

   In the document window, the insertion point is positioned between the two opening brackets in front of the word "Data". The outer bracket represents the beginning of the **Chapter** element. The inner bracket represents the beginning of the **Head** element.

   [[Data Communications]

   └── Insertion point

   In the lower left corner of your FrameMaker window, the status bar shows that you are currently in the **Chapter** element.

   Status bar — Flow: A E: Chapter
   Element name ────┘

2. Click anywhere within the title text "Data Communications" in the document window.

   [[Data Communications]

   Insertion point ──┘

   In the document window, the insertion point is positioned inside the **Head** element.

   In the **Structure** View, the insertion point is to the right of the **Head** element bubble. The hollow triangle indicates that you are neither at the beginning nor the end of the **Head** element.

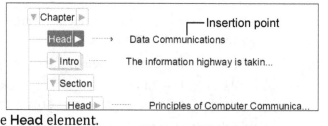

   The status bar displays the nesting of elements at the current position (the cursor is within the **Head** element, which is within the **Chapter** element.

   Status bar— Flow: A E: Chapter > Head
   Element name ┘

   In the **Structure** View, the position indicator is shaped like a triangle.

Depending on its location, the triangle can appear as follows:

The insertion point is:

At the beginning of the element

In the middle of the element

At the end of the element

3. Press the **right-arrow** key to move the cursor, one character at a time, to the end of the **Head** element. The arrow in the **Structure View** changes to reflect the end of the element (▶|).

4. Press the **left-arrow** key to move the cursor, one character at a time, to the beginning of the **Head** element. The arrow in the **Structure View** changes to reflect the start of the element (|▶).

5. Press the **left-arrow** key to move the cursor outside of the **Head** element and back into the **Chapter** element.

Exercise 5:   Positioning the insertion point in the Structure View

In this exercise you will use the arrow keys to navigate within the **Structure View**.

1. Click above the first **Head** element in the **Structure View** (if not already there from the previous exercise).

2. Hold down the **Ctrl + Alt** keys and press the **down-arrow** key, twice.

The insertion point moves down to each same-level element in the document. It stops first at the **Intro** element and secondly at the **Section** element, since they are both sibling elements.

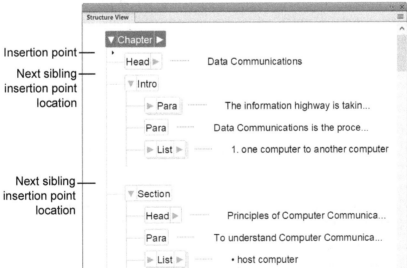

3. Hold down the **Ctrl + Alt** keys and press the **up-arrow** key twice, to return to where you started above the **Head** bubble.

4. Click above the first **Section** element, on the line descending from the **Chapter** element.

5. Press the **down-arrow** key several times. Note that the insertion moves line by line down through the document view.

6. Practice using the **left-arrow** and **right-arrow** keys to move character by character through the document view.

    This behavior makes viewing the element boundaries significant, in that you have many locations within the structure view that you would otherwise need to use your mouse to position the cursor. With the element boundaries on, moving left and right via the cursor keys is an efficient way to move through complex structures like lists and tables.

Collapsing and expanding elements

Collapsing elements in the **Structure View** helps to keep the **Structure View** compact, making it easier to scroll through the structure to work with other elements. You can expand elements, as needed. When an element is collapsed, all of its children move up and behind the parent element bubble. Element content in the document window is not affected.

Elements can be collapsed and expanded by clicking once on the right-facing arrow symbol (▶) in the element bubble, to the left of the element name to expand the element or once on the downward-facing arrow symbol (▼) to collapse the element.

After you collapse or expand an element, the symbol in the element bubble changes to reflect the status of the element, right-facing arrow symbol (▶) for collapsed elements and downward-facing arrow symbol (▼) for expanded elements.

 You can also access additional expand and collapse options by right-clicking an element bubble, or expand/collapse current element and its siblings by shift clicking the arrow icon on the left edge of an element bubble.

Exercise 6:   Collapsing and expanding elements

In this exercise, you will practice the various ways of collapsing and expanding elements in the **Structure View**.

1. Scroll to the **Intro** element at the beginning of the structure.

2. On the left side of the **Intro** element bubble, click the downward-facing arrow symbol (▼).

    The **Intro** element is collapsed and a right-facing arrow symbol (▶) displays.

3. In the **Structure View**, locate the **Section** element that follows the **Intro** element.

4. On the left side of the **Section** element bubble, click the downward-facing arrow symbol (▼).

    The **Section** element collapses and a right-facing arrow symbol (▶) displays.

    The element can now be expanded by clicking on the **Section** element right-facing arrow symbol (▶).

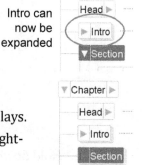

The expand/collapse symbol (►) is red because Section contains a child element with a validation error you will fix in a future exercise. You can ignore the red expand symbol for now.

5. On the left side of the **Intro** element, click the right-facing arrow symbol (►).

    The **Intro** element expands and a downward-facing arrow symbol (▼) displays.

6. On the left side of the **Section** element, click the right-facing arrow symbol (►).

    The **Section** element expands and a downward-facing arrow symbol (▼) displays.

 The expand/collapse symbol (▼) for Section is no longer red because the child of Section is invalid, not the Section element itself.

Viewing Attributes

Attributes provide a way to store descriptive information for an element. For example, in this document, the **Chapter** element contains an attribute to store the author's name.

An element can contain zero or more attributes. These attributes display in the **Structure View**, directly beneath the element bubble. An element with attributes will have expand/collapse symbols that behave like the expand/collapse symbols in the previous section.

After you hide or show an element's attributes, the symbol in the element bubble changes to reflect what the next click will do. However, attributes have three potential states, which you will see in the following exercises.

Exercise 7:   Viewing all attributes

In this exercise, you will use the **Attribute Display Options** dialog box to display all attributes in the **Structure View**.

1. Select **View > Attribute Display Options** in the main menu.

    The **Attribute Display Options** dialog box displays.

2. Select (turn on) the **All Attributes** radio button and click the **Set** button.

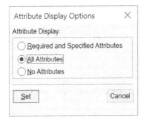

The **Structure View** displays all attributes.

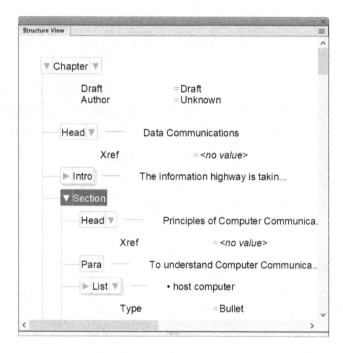

 Exercise 8:   Showing and hiding attributes for individual elements

In this exercise, you will hide the attributes for an individual element in the **Structure View**.

1. Scroll to the **Chapter** element at the very top of the **Structure View**.

2. On the right side of the **Chapter** element, click the downward-facing arrow symbol (▼).

    The attributes are hidden and a right-facing arrow symbol (▶) displays.

3. On the right side of the **List** element, click the downward-facing arrow symbol (▼).

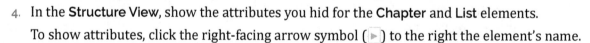

    The attribute is hidden and a right-facing arrow symbol (▶) displays.

4. In the **Structure View**, show the attributes you hid for the **Chapter** and **List** elements.

    To show attributes, click the right-facing arrow symbol (▶) to the right the element's name.

The Element Catalog

The **Element Catalog** (displayed in the panel labeled **Elements**) is a context-sensitive list of elements you can use in a document. The elements displayed in the **Element Catalog** can change, according to the location of the insertion point in the document. The **Element Catalog** also contains buttons used to manipulate elements.

The process of using the **Element Catalog** is called "Guided Editing", because the **Element Catalog** guides the user from the beginning to the end of a document by helping the user to select valid elements. A valid element will have a symbol next to its name in the **Element Catalog**.

Symbol	Meaning
✓	Element is valid at current location. If you insert it, parent will be valid up to insertion point.
✓+	Element is an inclusion. Listed inclusions are valid anywhere within current element and its descendants.
√	Element is valid in current element. If you insert it, the current element will be correct, but incomplete up to the insertion point.
?	Element can validly replace the element following the insertion point, or selected element. Replacement makes elements after it invalid.
No symbol	Element is invalid at current location.

Exercise 9: Opening the Element Catalog

In this exercise, you will open the **Element Catalog** and move the insertion point to observe how the **Element Catalog** changes, showing the elements valid at the current insertion point.

1. In the document window, place your cursor directly under the chapter element.

2. If not visible, display the Element Catalog by clicking the **Element Catalog** icon in the Structured Access toolbar. or by using the View > Pods > Element Catalog command.

    The **Element Catalog** displays.

Depending on your Element Catalog options (⚙) you may see a different set of elements available in the Element Catalog. You will set these options in the next exercise.

3. Locate the first **Section** element and click below the first **Para** element in the section.

You may see a contextual list like the one shown here, or a longer list that includes elements not valid at the current location. Each have their advantages, which you'll investigate in the next exercise.

4. Place the insertion point in several other locations in the **Structure View** and see if there is a change to the elements displayed in the **Element Catalog.**

Changing the Element Catalog display options

You can change what is displayed in the **Element Catalog.** by clicking on the Options button (⚙).

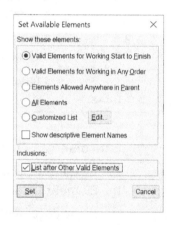

In your own work you might at times find each of these options useful, but in this workbook you should keep the options as listed here. These settings allow you to learn about your content model, without cluttering up your catalog.

The **Inclusions: List after Other Valid Elements** option moves infrequently used items (defined in the EDD as Inclusions) to the end of your list, further highlighting the elements most often used in your system.

Exercise 10: Changing the Element Catalog display

In this exercise, you will display all elements in the **Element Catalog.**

1. In the **Structure View,** click just above the **Head** element, on the line descending from the **Chapter** element.1

The **Element Catalog** displays only those elements valid at the insertion point.

2. In the **Element Catalog**, click the Options button (⚙), or select **Element > Set Available Elements** in the main menu).

   The **Set Available Elements** dialog box displays.

3. Select (turn on) the **All Elements** radio button and click on the **Set** button.

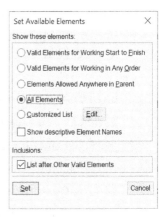

The **Element Catalog** now lists all of the elements available in the document. The valid elements (inclusions, in this case) are listed first.

 For the most control, set the inclusions to list after other valid elements. This gives you a sorted list of most likely elements to be used at the top of the catalog, followed by a sorted list of valid elements that are used less frequently. When viewing all elements, the elements not valid at a given location are shown in a third sorted list below the inclusions.

Optional Exercise

The following exercise enables you to enhance your FrameMaker skills and to explore additional features. The steps are intentionally brief and require more independent thought on your part.

 Exercise 11: Creating a customized element list

In this exercise, you will create a customized list in the **Element Catalog**.

1. From the **Element Catalog**, select the **Options** button.

2. Click on **Customized List** radio button and click the **Edit** button.

   The **Customize List of Available Elements** dialog box displays.

3. From the **Customize List of Available Elements** dialog, move **Chapter** to the **Show** list.

4. Move the **Intro, List, Para, Section, Term, Item,** and **Head** elements to the **Show** scroll list:

5. Select the **Section** element in the **Show** scroll list.

6. Click the **Move Up** button twice, to move the **Section** element below the **Intro** element.

7. Using **Move Up** and **Move Down** buttons, rearrange the elements as shown on the right.

8. Click the **Set** button to close the **Customize List of Available Elements** dialog.

9. Click the **Set** button to close the **Set Available Elements** dialog.

The **Element Catalog** displays your customized list. As you reposition the insertion point, all of these elements continue to display—with symbols indicating their validity or no symbol when invalid.

10. Select **File > Save** from the main menu, and then **File > Close**.

Structure Terms

This section is a quick-reference list of element terms and relationships.

Refer to these definitions until you become more familiar with the structuring concepts and terms of FrameMaker.

Ancestors	In the element hierarchy, all elements that are above a given element
Attributes	Additional information used to describe an element, such as a list type or graphic reference number
Child elements	Elements that are contained by or subordinate to a higher (parent) element
Descendants	In the element hierarchy, all elements that are subordinate to a parent element
Element	A structural unit of a document
Element boundaries	Square brackets in the document window that mark where each element begins and ends
Element boundaries as Tags	Brackets with element names in the document window that mark where each element begins and ends
Element bubbles	Rectangular "bubble" shapes in the Structure View that contain the name of an element. The vertical and horizontal connecting lines show how bubbles are related.
Element hierarchy	The structure that defines which elements are above, subordinate to, or equal to others
Element Catalog display	Displays a configurable list of elements that can be added at the insertion point along with information about the effect of their addition on the structure's validity.
Parent element	An element that contains subordinate elements
Sibling elements	Children of the same parent element.
Text snippet	The beginning text of a text-containing element, located in the Structure View to the right of the element bubble.
Valid document	A document in which all elements and their attributes conform to their defined content requirements.
Invalid document	A document that has one or more areas in which correct structuring procedures have not been followed.
Validation	Using the Element Validation tool to locate and fix invalid and incomplete elements, or attributes.

Chapter 4: Editing Text

Introduction

In this module, you will become familiar with the text-editing features and capabilities of FrameMaker.

Using these features, you can enter and manipulate text efficiently, and automatically ensure your document adheres to typographic conventions, such as quotation marks and extra spaces.

Module Objectives

In this module you will learn how to:

- Enter text, including special characters.
- Select and deselect text.
- Cut, copy, paste, move, and delete text.
- Undo changes.
- Use **Smart Spaces** and **Smart Quotes**.
- Use the **Revert to Saved** feature.
- Use the **Spelling Checker**.
- Use the **Find/Change** command.

Adding and Deleting Text

To add text to a FrameMaker document, click in the text flow where you want to type the new text, then begin typing. To change text, click inside a word, and delete or add in new text or letters. Replace text by highlighting the old text and typing in new text. Any highlighted text is automatically replaced with the next keyboard action.

To delete text, highlight the text and press the **Delete** or **Backspace** key, or select **Edit > Clear** from the main menu.

 Exercise 1:   (Review) Adding and deleting text

In this exercise, you will turn on the borders and text symbols, zoom the document to 120%, fit the window to the page, and insert and delete text in the document window.

1. Open `Chapter04.fm` from the `AuthClassFiles2020` directory.
2. If borders are not visible, select **View > Borders** from the main menu.
3. If element boundaries are not visible, select **View > Element Boundaries** from the main menu.
4. Set the document zoom to **120%**.

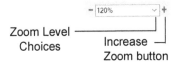

5. Place the insertion point at the end of the first paragraph; between the period and the closing element boundary.

[[The information highway is taking the world by storm. Everyday thousands of experienced and novice computer users are 'taking the on-ramp' and 'surfing' through tens of thousands of files, often meeting and chatting with users half-way around the world. Many of these info-hungry 'interneters' haven't a clue as to how their data is moving on the 'net'.]]

Insertion point

6. Press the **space bar** once and type:

   `This paper provides a brief overview of the basics of how this data actually moves from one computer to another.`

7. At the bottom of page 1 in the document window, locate the paragraph following the heading "**Receiving Computer**".

[[Receiving Computer]] [The receiving computer is often simply what's called a dumb terminal, which is a keyboard, a display monitor, and some sort of communications

8. Place the insertion point at the end of the "Receiving Computer" paragraph (on page 2); between the period after *expansion slot* and the closing element boundary.

port. Or it may be a personal computer that emulates the characteristics of a dumb terminal through the use of special software and a board installed in an expansion slot.]

Insertion point

9. Press the **space bar** once and type:

   `Even today's hand-held PDAs (personal data assistants) which fit in the palm of your hand, communicate with networks world-wide through radio frequency and infrared connections.`

10. On page 2 in the document window, locate the paragraph following the heading "**Data**".

11. Click to place the cursor insertion point in the last sentence, before the semi-colon (;) in front of the word "all".

[[Data]] [This is the whole reason for establishing a network-to transmit data of any kind. How is data represented in a network? The combination of digital bits that represent computer characters move in a channel inside each computer that handles transmission. This internal channel (also called a bUs) carries the data to a communications or serial port which may be physically connected to another computer or to a device which communicates to another device of it's type; all which use distinct connection media.]

Insertion point

12. Hold mouse button down and drag to highlight the phrase; "; all which use distinct connection media"

[[Data]] [This is the whole reason for establishing a network-to transmit data of any kind. How is data represented in a network? The combination of digital bits that represent computer characters move in a channel inside each computer that handles transmission. This internal channel (also called a bUs) carries the data to a communications or serial port which may be physically connected to another computer or to a device which communicates to another device of it's type; all which use distinct connection media.]

Delete highlighted phrase

13. Press the **Delete** button.

14. Select **File > Save** from the main menu.

Selecting and Changing

You may select text using any of the following techniques:

- Click and drag the mouse cursor (I-beam) over the text you want to select.
- Double-click a word.
- Double-click a word, press the **Shift** key, then click at the end of additional words.
- Use a keyboard shortcut to select text.

Once text is selected (highlighted), the first typed character replaces the entire highlighted selection. You can deselect text by clicking somewhere else in the document window or in **Structure View**.

 If you drag the I-beam (mouse cursor) over an element boundary, FrameMaker will select the entire element.

Exercise 2:   (Review) Selecting and changing text

In this exercise, you will practice various ways of selecting text, as well as replacing selected text.

1. On page 1 in the document window, double-click the word "Data" in the heading "**Data Communications**".

   The word "**Data**" is selected (highlighted).

   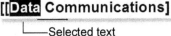
   └──Selected text

2. Type: `Computer`

   The selected text is deleted and the new text is inserted.

3. On page 1 in the document window, locate the paragraph following the heading "**Receiving Computer**".

4. In the paragraph's second line, select the words "some sort of".

   [[Receiving Computer]] [The receiving computer is often simply what's called a dumb terminal, which is a keyboard, a display monitor, and some sort of communications

5. Type: `a`

   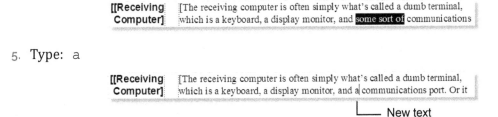
   └── New text

   The selected text is deleted and the new text is inserted.

6. Select **File > Save** from the main menu.

Clear and Undo commands

The **Clear** command deletes selected text, elements or attributes, just like pressing the **Delete** or **Back** (Backspace) key. When you use the **Clear** command, the selected item is not put on the clipboard for later pasting.

The **Undo** command allows you to undo the immediately preceding action. This is helpful if you change your mind while editing a document.

 Exercise 3:   Using Clear and Undo

In this exercise, you will use the **Clear** command to delete some text and immediately undo the deletion.

1. Select any text within its element boundaries.

2. Select **Edit > Clear** from the main menu.

   The text is removed from the document.

3. Select **Edit > Undo** from the main menu.

   The **Clear** command is undone and the text redisplays.

Cutting, Copying and Pasting

To move text or elements, make a selection, cut it, and paste it into a new location. When you cut an item, the item is placed on the clipboard. The item can be pasted at another location in the same or different document. The item stays on the clipboard until you cut or copy something else.

To copy text or elements to a new location, select the item, and use the **Copy** and **Paste** commands. When you use the **Copy** command, the selected item is not removed from the document when it is copied to the clipboard.

 Exercise 4:   Cutting, copying, and pasting text

In this exercise, you will move and duplicate text, using the **Cut**, **Copy**, and **Paste** commands.

1. On page 2 in the document window, locate the second paragraph that follows the heading "Receiving Computer".

2. Select the entire paragraph but not the element boundaries.

3. Select **Edit > Cut** from the main menu.

   The content inside the element is cut and placed on the clipboard.

> [Any electrical impulse that must travel along an analog communication channel must first be modulated. This converts it from a digital signal into an analog one. When the signal reaches the end of the network, it must then be "de-modulated, converted back to a digital signal that a computer can understand. This is the function of a modem]]

 If you wanted to move the content as its own paragraph, you would have selected the boundaries, or simply clicked on the element in the **Structure View**.

4. On page 4 in the document window, place the insertion point at the end of the last paragraph in the document, between the period and the closing element boundary.

5. Press the **space bar**.

6. Select **Edit > Paste** from the main menu.

   The text is added to the current paragraph at the insertion point.

7. Highlight only the first two empty element boundaries, where the paragraph in step 2 existed, and press the **Delete** key.

8. On page 2 in the document window, locate "Table 1. **Connection Devices**".

9. In the second body row, double-click the word "line" to select it.

10. Select **Edit > Copy** from the main.

    The text is copied and placed on the Clipboard.

11. In the third body row, place the insertion point after the word "telephone".

12. Press the **space bar** once.

13. Select **Edit > Paste** from the main menu.

    The word "line" is pasted at the insertion point.

14. Select **File > Save** from the main menu.

[Data can be in either a digital or analog format, and the two are quite different. Digitally formatted data is either on or off, 1 or 0. An analog signal, on the other hand, may consist of a wide range of values.]]]]

└─ Insertion point

[Data can be in either a digital or analog format, and the two are quite different. Digitally formatted data is either on or off, 1 or 0. An analog signal, on the other hand, may consist of a wide range of values. Any electrical impulse that must travel along an analog communication channel must first be modulated. This converts it from a digital signal into an analog one. When the signal reaches the end of the network, it must then be "de-modulated, converted back to a digital signal that a computer can understand. This is the function of a modem.]]]]

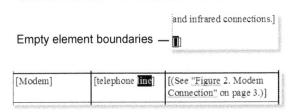

and infrared connections.]

Empty element boundaries ─

[Modem]	[telephone **line**]	[(See "Figure 2. Modem Connection" on page 3.)]

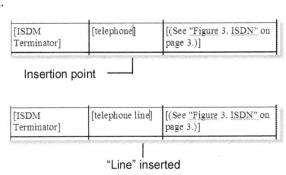

[ISDM Terminator]	[telephone]	[(See "Figure 3. ISDN" on page 3.)]

Insertion point ─

[ISDM Terminator]	[telephone line]	[(See "Figure 3. ISDN" on page 3.)]

"Line" inserted

Smart Spaces and Smart Quotes

When enabled, Smart Spaces:

- Prevents you from typing more than one consecutive space.
- Automatically deletes the extra space remaining when you delete a word.
- Does not remove any extra spaces typed before **Smart Spaces** is turned on (use **Find/Change** or **Spelling Checker** to identify **2 or more consecutive spaces in existing content**)

Smart Quotes:

- Automatically curves quotation marks when enabled.
  - "example" not "example"

    and
  - 'example' not 'example'

- Does not change any quotation marks typed before **Smart Quotes** is turned on (use **Find/Change** or **Spelling Checker** to find and change existing quotation marks).

The following table lists keyboard combinations for inserting straight quotes when **Smart Quotes** is on and curved quotes when **Smart Quotes** is off, as well as spaces of various widths.

To Type:	Use:
' (straight single quotation mark)	Ctrl-'
" (straight double quotation mark), when Smart Quotes is on	Esc "
' (left single quotation mark, when Smart Quotes is off, or when typed in dialog box)	Ctrl-q Shift-t
' (right single quotation mark, when Smart Quotes is off, or when typed in dialog box)	Ctrl-q Shift-u
" (left double quotation mark, when Smart Quotes is off, or when typed in dialog box)	Ctrl-q Shift-r
" (right double quotation mark, when Smart Quotes is off, or when typed in dialog box)	Ctrl-q Shift-s
Em space	Esc space m
En space	Esc space n
Nonbreaking space	Esc space h
Numeric space (width of font's zero)	Esc space 1

 Exercise 5: Using Smart Spaces

In this exercise, you will enter spaces with **Smart Spaces** on and then add spaces with **Smart Spaces** off.

1. Place the insertion point anywhere between the text.
2. Press the **space bar** several times.

   Because **Smart Spaces** is turned on, the extras spaces are not added.

3. Select **Format > Document > Text Options** from the main menu.

The **Text Options** dialog box displays.

4. Select the **Smart Spaces** check box to turn **Smart Spaces** off, and click the **Apply** button.

5. With the insertion point still in the same place, press the **space bar** several times.

    With **Smart Spaces** turned off, extra spaces are added.

6. Select **Format > Document > Text Options** from the main menu.

    The **Text Options** dialog box displays again.

7. Click in the **Smart Spaces** check box and click the **Apply** button.

    Notice that turning on **Smart Spaces** does not remove the extra spaces already in the document.

8. Press the **Backspace** key, once.

    Because **Smart Spaces** is on, all spaces, except one, are deleted.

9. On page 1 in the document window, in the first sentence of the first paragraph, double-click the word "highway".

    [[The information highway is taking the world by storm. Everyday thousands of experienced and novice computer users are 'taking the on-ramp' and 'surfing' through tens of thousands of files, often meeting and chatting with users half-way around the world. Many of these info-hungry 'interneters' haven't a clue as to how their data is moving on the 'net'. This paper provides a brief overview of the basics of how this data actually moves from one computer to another.]

10. Press the **Backspace** or **Delete** key, once.

    Because **Smart Spaces** is on, the word "highway" and the extra space are deleted.

    [[The information is taking the world by storm. Everyday thousands of experienced and novice computer users are 'taking the on-ramp' and 'surfing' through tens of thousands of files, often meeting and chatting with users half-way around the world. Many of these info-hungry 'interneters' haven't a clue as to how their data is moving on the 'net'. This paper provides a brief overview of the basics of how this data actually moves from one computer to another.]

11. Select **Edit > Undo Clear** from the main menu.

    The word "highway" and the extra space reappear.

Exercise 6:   Using Smart Quotes

In this exercise, you will insert quotation marks with the **Smart Quotes** option off, and then insert quotation marks with the **Smart Quotes** option on.

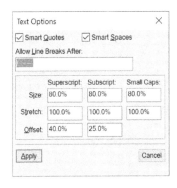

1. Select **Format > Document > Text Options** from the main menu.

    The **Text Options** dialog box displays.

2. Click the **Smart Quotes** check box (check mark removed) to turn off **Smart Quotes**, and click the **Apply** button.

3. On page 1 in the document window, locate the first sentence following the heading "Receiving Computer".

4. In the sentence, locate the phrase "dumb terminal".

    [Receiving Computer]   [The receiving computer is often simply what's called a dumb terminal, which is a keyboard, a display monitor, and some sort of communications

5. Type a quotation mark before the word "dumb" and after the word "terminal".

Straight quotation marks are inserted.

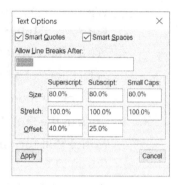

[[Receiving Computer]] [The receiving computer is often simply what's called a "dumb terminal", which is a keyboard, a display monitor, and a communications port. Or it

6. Select **Format > Document > Text Options** from the main menu.

   The **Text Options** dialog box displays.

7. Click in the **Smart Quotes** check box (check mark displaying) and click the **Apply** button.

   Notice that turning on **Smart Quotes** does not change the straight quotation marks already inserted.

8. Delete the two straight quotation marks you already inserted.

9. Insert quotations marks around the phrase "dumb terminal", again.

   This time, curved quotation marks are inserted.

10. Select **File > Save** from the main menu.

Special Characters

In addition to regular text, you can add special characters. These include widely recognized symbols such as the **em dash** (—) and the **trademark symbol**(™).

 To download a PDF showing how to insert the most popular special characters in FrameMaker, see the post at http://www.techcommtools.com/insert-infinity-char/

 Exercise 7: Adding special characters

In this exercise, you will insert an **em dash** in your document.

1. On page 2 in the document window, locate the first paragraph following the heading "**Data**".

2. Select the hyphen (-) in the first sentence.

3. Press **Backspace** or **Delete** key to delete the hyphen (-).

4. Use the following keyboard shortcut to add an em dash after the word

[[Data]] [This is the whole reason for establishing a network-to transmit data of any kind. How is data represented in a network? The combination of digital bits that represent computer characters move in a channel inside each computer that handles transmission. This internal channel (also called a bUs) carries the data to a communications or serial port which may be physically connected to another computer or to a device which communicates to another device of it's type; all which use distinct connection media.]

"network":
```
Ctrl+q Q
```

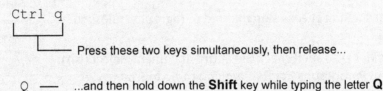

Tip: The above shortcut is actually two keystrokes:

```
Ctrl q
```
—— Press these two keys simultaneously, then release...

Q —— ...and then hold down the **Shift** key while typing the letter **Q**

An em dash (—) appears after the word "network".

5. Select **File > Save**, and then **File > Close** from the main menu.

[[Data]] [This is the whole reason for establishing a network—to transmit data of any kind. How is data represented in a network? The combination of digital bits that represent computer characters move in a channel inside each computer that handles transmission. This internal channel (also called a bUs) carries the data to a communications or serial port which may be physically connected to another computer or to a device which communicates to another device of it's type; all which use distinct connection media.]

Spelling Checker

When you spell-check a document, FrameMaker compares words in the document against four dictionaries:

- Main dictionary
- Site dictionary
- Personal dictionary
- Document dictionary

The **Spelling Checker** window allows you to control the way FrameMaker does its spell checking.

As you spell check, you can add custom words to the Personal and Document dictionaries. The Main and Site dictionaries cannot be modified by end-users.

In addition to misspellings, you can check for many common typing errors including:

- Repeated words
- Extra spaces
- Unusual hyphenation or capitalization

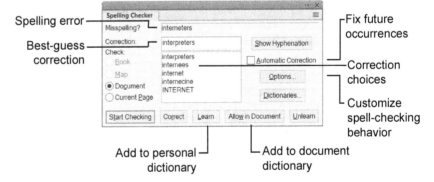

The **Spelling Checker**:

- Begins at the insertion point and goes forward.

- Circles back to the top and continues forward.
- Indicates "**Spelling OK**" in the upper-left corner of **Spelling Checker** window when all the errors are corrected.
- Marks paragraphs as having been checked.
- Additional spelling checks skip marked paragraphs unless they are edited.

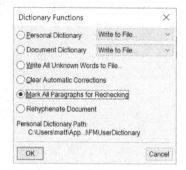

To force FrameMaker to spell check the entire document, select (turn on) the **Mark All Paragraphs For Rechecking** radio button in the **Dictionary Functions** dialog box, and click the **OK** button.

Exercise 8:   Using the Spelling Checker

In this exercise, you will spell check your document, correcting errors, and adding words to your dictionaries.

1. Open `Chapter04.fm` from the `AuthClassFiles2020` directory.

   a. Select **File > Open** from the main menu.

      The **Open** dialog box displays.

   b. If necessary, change to the `AuthClassFiles2020` directory.

   c. Double-click on `Chapter04.fm`.

      The document displays in the document window.

2. Select **Edit > Spelling Checker** from the main menu.

   The **Spelling Checker** dialog box displays.

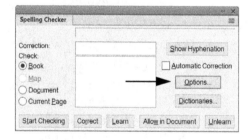

3. Click on the **Options** button.

   The **Preferences** dialog box displays.

4. Click on **Spelling Options**.

5. If necessary, turn the **Preferences** settings on or off (select or deselect the check boxes), as shown above.

6. Click the **OK** button.

7. On page 1 in the document window, place the insertion point at beginning of "**Computer**" in the document title.

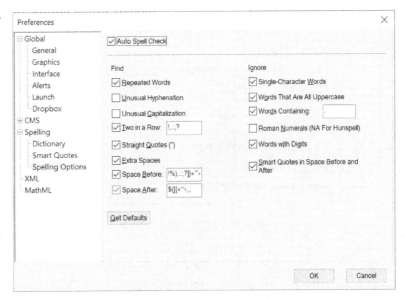

8. In the **Spelling Checker** window, click **Start Checking**.

   The misspelled word "termnal" is highlighted. In the **Correction** field, the suggested correction, "terminal", is correct.

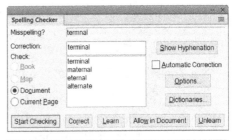

9. Click the **Correct** button.

   The "termnal" misspelling is corrected and the **PDAs** error is highlighted.

   The word "**PDAs**" is valid but not found in the FrameMaker dictionaries. However, it can be added to your personal dictionary or the document dictionary.

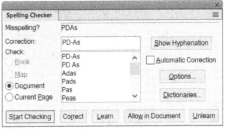

10. Click the **Allow in Document** button to add "PDAs" to your personal dictionary.

    An Undo alert displays. Click the **OK** button to clear the alert.

11. Click the **Start Checking** button to find the next spelling error.

    An extra space is found and the correction of removing the space before "?" is correct.

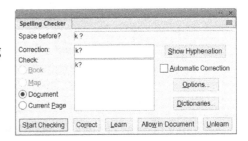

12. Click the **Correct** button.

    The word "bus" is found in the FrameMaker
    dictionaries and is valid, but the upper-case "U" in
    "bUs" needs to be corrected. In the **Correction** field,
    "bus" is correct.

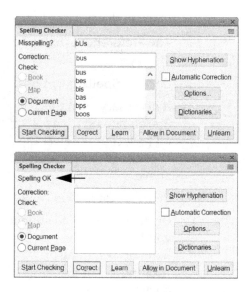

13. Click the **Correct** button.

14. Click the **Correct** button until the **Spelling Checker**
    dialog box reports "**Spelling OK**" in the upper-left
    corner.

15. Close the **Spelling Checker**.

    You can close the panel either by selecting the Close
    button ( ) or by right-clicking on the Spelling
    Checker tab and selecting **Close** or **Close Tab Group**.

16. Select **File > Save** from the main menu, and then **File > Close**.

Find and Change

The **Find** and **Change** command can:

- Search for text, elements, formats, tables, graphics, and more.

- Replace what you find with
  text, or anything that can be
  copied to the clipboard.

When searching for text, you can
use the following controls:

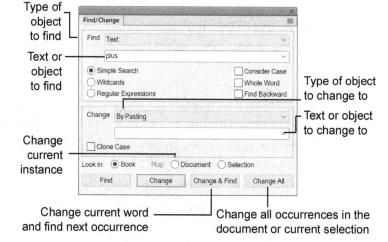

- **Consider Case** - takes into
  account the case
  (upper and/or lower) of the
  text typed in the Find field

- **Whole Word** - determines
  whether or not the word to
  find is part of a larger word
  or is actually the whole word.

- **Wildcards** - uses the "*"
  (asterisk) or "?" (question mark) wildcards as part of the find text. The "*" indicates zero or
  more characters. The "?" indicates exactly one character.

- **Find Backward** - searches text backward from the current cursor location.

To make the change, click either the **Change**, **Change & Find**, or **Change All** button.

Exercise 9: Finding text

In this exercise, you will turn the **Consider Case** and **Whole Word** options on and off to find text.

1. Navigate to the `Class` directory and open `mod04.fm`, if necessary.

2. Select **Edit > Find/Change** from the main menu.

   The **Find/Change** dialog box displays with the **Simple Search** radio button selected.

3. If not already selected, click the **Find** menu to select **Text:** from the menu.

4. In the **Find** text box, type: `modem`

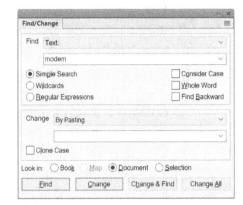

5. If not already off, turn off **Consider Case**, **Whole Word**, and **Find Backward**, by ensuring the check boxes are unchecked.

6. Click the find **Find** button.

   The first occurrence of "modem" is highlighted in the document.

7. Click the find **Find** button again.

   The next occurrence of "modem" is highlighted in the document. Because **Whole Word** is turned off, an occurrence of "modem" is found in the word "Modems".

8. Click the find **Find** button again.

   The next occurrence is highlighted because **Consider Case** is turned off, and an occurrence with different capitalization is found.

9. Click in **Whole Word** check box.

10. Click the find **Find** button a few times.

    Notice that "Modems" in Figure 2 is skipped.

11. Turn off **Whole Word** and turn on **Consider Case**.

12. Click the find **Find** button a few times.

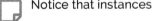
Notice that instances of "Modems", and "Modem" are skipped.

Exercise 10: Changing text

In this exercise, you will find all occurrences of "data" and change them to "information".

1. Turn off **Consider Case**.
2. Delete "modem" in the **Find** text box and type: `data`
3. In the **Change** text box, type: `information`
4. Enable the **Clone Case** check box.

   Because **Consider Case** is off, the word "data", with any case, will be found.

   Because **Clone Case** is on, when you change "data" to "information", the case will be cloned.
5. On page 1, place the insertion point left of the word "Data" in the second paragraph.
6. Click the **Find** button.

   The word "Data" is highlighted.
7. Click the **Change** button.

   The word "Information" replaces "Data".
8. Click the **Find** button.

   The word "data" is highlighted.
9. Click the **Change** button.

   The word "information" replaces "data" in the list.
10. Click the **Find** button.

    The next word "data" is highlighted.
11. Click the **Change & Find** button.

    The word "information" replaces "data", and the next occurrence is automatically found.
12. Continue clicking the **Change & Find** button until you see the alert "**Not found**".
13. Click the **OK** button to dismiss the alert.
14. Right-click on the **Find/Change** tab at the top of the dialog box and select **Close** from the menu.
15. Select **File > Save** from the main menu, and then select **File > Close**.

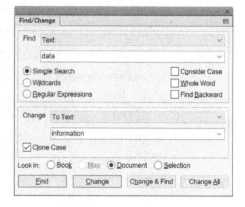

Chapter 5: Editing Structure

Introduction

In this module, you will use the **Element Catalog** to insert new elements, change existing elements, wrap elements around existing text, unwrap, merge, and split elements. In addition, you will learn to recognize invalid elements in the **Structure View** and correct them.

Module Objectives

In this module, you'll learn how to:

- Insert new elements.
- Type text in new elements.
- Wrap elements around existing text.
- Change elements.
- Merge two or more elements into one.
- Split an element into two.
- Unwrap an element.
- Recognize incorrectly placed and missing elements.

Manipulating Elements

In the following exercises, you will learn how to manipulate elements by inserting, changing, wrapping, moving, and deleting them.

Inserting elements and adding text

When you want to add new content in a document, such as a heading, you insert the appropriate element first and then enter the text.

In the first part of this chapter you'll enter things a bit more slowly than you might expect.

Don't worry, in the second half of the chapter we'll speed things up by taking advantage of automation available in the template used to create this document.

 Exercise 1: Inserting elements

In this exercise, you will begin to edit a structured document, inserting elements using the **Element Catalog** and using the **Structure View** to guide you.

1. From the `AuthClass2020` directory, open `Chapter05.fm`.
2. Make the borders and element boundaries visible from the **View** menu, if not already visible.

3. Change the elements displayed in the **Element Catalog** to **Valid Elements for Working Start to Finish.**

   a. Select **Element > Set Available Elements** from the main menu.

      The **Set Available Elements** dialog box displays.

   b. Select (turn on) the **Valid Elements for Working Start to Finish** radio button, if not already selected.

   c. Click the **Set** button.

      The **Set Available Elements** dialog box closes.

   d. (Optional, but recommended) Ensure that **Inclusions: List after Other Valid Elements** is selected.

4. Ensure that the **Structure View** and **Element Catalog** are visible.

   a. Click the **Structure View** button in the main menu.

      Structure View

   b. Click the **Element Catalog** button in the main menu.

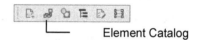

      Element Catalog

5. Arrange the screen so you can see all three windows; the document window, the **Structure View**, and the **Element Catalog**. Here is one suggestion for arranging your windows and pods.

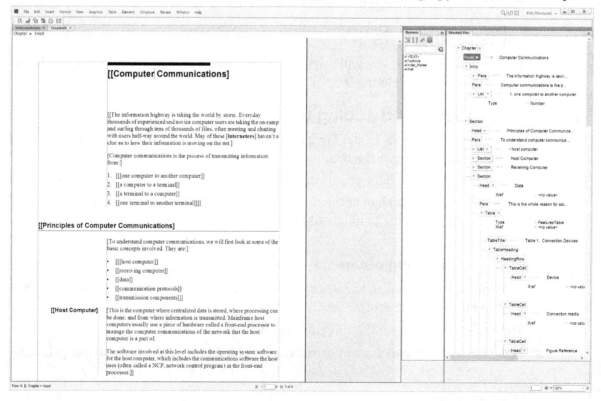

6. On page 1 in the document window, place the insertion point anywhere in the heading "Computer Communications".

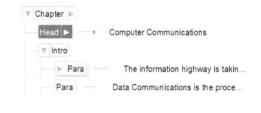

By clicking in this first **Head** element, you have positioned the cursor in both the document window and the **Structure View** near the beginning of the document.

The triangle icon in front of the **Head** snippet shows that the cursor is somewhere in the middle of the **Head** element.

7. Collapse the **Intro** element and **Section** elements below the **Chapter** element in the **Structure View**.

8. Click below the collapsed **Section** element in the **Structure View**, on the line descending from the **Chapter** element.

9. Select the **Section** element in the **Element Catalog** and click the **Insert** button.

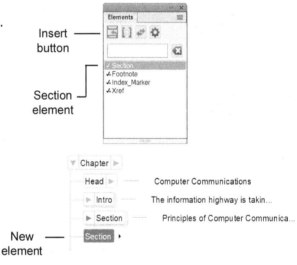

Insert button

Section element

A new **Section** element displays in the **Structure View**.

New element

Element boundaries (square brackets) for the **Section** element display in the document window.

[Data can be in either a digital or analog format, and the two are quite different. Digitally formatted data is either on or off, 1 or 0. An analog signal, on the other hand, may consist of a wide range of values.]]]

 If you automatically get a **Head** element inserted at this step, delete it and go to **Element>New Element Options**. Deselect the **Allow Automatic Insertion of Children option**. You'll enable this feature in a later lesson.

Exercise 2:   Adding a child element

In this exercise, you will add child elements to the **Section** element and enter text into the new elements.

1. If not already there, position your cursor on the right side of the **Section** element in the **Structure View**.

    An arrow displays on the right side of the **Section** element bubble.

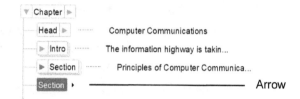

2. Select **Head** in the **Element Catalog** and click the **Insert** button.

    A bubble for the **Head** element displays under the **Section** element in the **Structure View**.

    Take note of the square at the end of the **Section** element, indicating that a required element is missing.

    Element boundaries (square brackets) display inside the **Section** element boundaries in the document window.

    The **Element Catalog** displays the elements valid in this **Head** element.

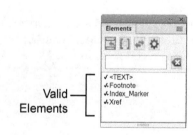

3. In the **Head** element, type: `Communication Protocols`

   In order to type, the insertion point (mouse click) must be to the right of the **Head** element bubble in **Structure View**.

   As you type, a text snippet displays the typed text to the right of the **Head** element bubble in the **Structure View**.

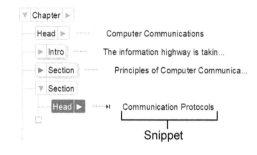

4. Position your cursor below the Head element in the **Structure View** as shown here, on the line descending from the **Section** element.

5. In the **Element Catalog**, select **Para** and click the **Insert** button.

6. The **Para** element displays under the **Head** element in the **Structure View**.

7. At the **Para** element, type: `Protocols are sets of rules. Many different protocols exist for different types of data transmission.`

In a later module, you will learn how to use the Return key as a shortcut to insert an element. For now, if you accidentally press Return, you can use the Undo command.

Exercise 3: Adding more elements

In this exercise, you will add a nested **Section** element to a **Section**.

1. Click below the **Para** element, on the line descending from the **Section** element, in the **Structure View**.

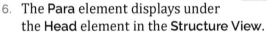

2. In the **Element Catalog**, select **Section** and click the **Insert** button.

   A new **Section** element displays, nested on the line underneath the previously inserted **Section** (parent) element.

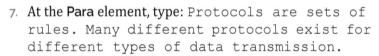

3. In the **Element Catalog**, select **Head** and click the **Insert** button.

4. Position your cursor to the right of the **Head** element and type:
   `Transmission Components`

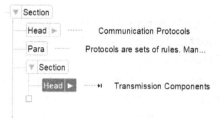

Since the **Head** element is designed to appear in the side-head area of the page, the text and its element boundaries appear towards the left side of the page in the document window.

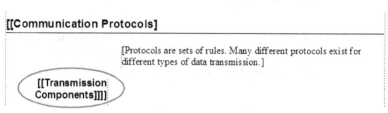

5. Move your cursor directly below the **Head** element.

6. Insert a **Para** element from the **Element Catalog**.

   The new **Para** element displays below the **Head** element.

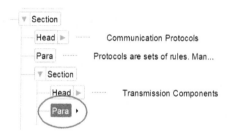

7. In the **Para** element, type:

   `Once all the computers are running successfully, the appropriate hardware components must be available. These include:`

Note that the first parts of a section have a rigid structure for both first and second level sections. After that initial pattern, the content model opens up. The next exercise will illustrate that point.

Exercise 4:   Adding a list element

In this exercise, you will add a **List** element and its descendants.

1. Click below the **Para** element in the **Structure View**, on the line descending from the **Section** element.

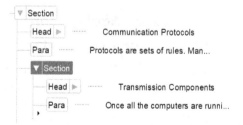

2. In the **Element Catalog**, select **List** and click the **Insert** button. The **List** element displays in the **Structure View**.

3. In the **Element Catalog**, select **Item** and click the **Insert** button.

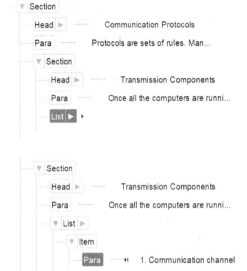

4. With the insertion point still to the right of the **Item** element, in the **Element Catalog**, select **Para** and click the **Insert** button.

   The **Para** element displays in the **Structure View**.

5. In the **Para** element, type:
   `Communication channel`

   Note that the item is automatically numbered.

 Notice the red square below the **Item** element, indicating that a required element is missing. The **List** element in this particular structured document requires at least two Item elements.

6. In the **Structure view**, place your cursor in the position needed to enter a sibling **Item** element.

   One way to get your cursor in this position is to click your right arrow key twice to move between the boundaries in your structure view.

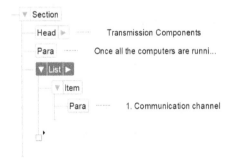

7. In the **Element Catalog**, select **Item** and click the **Insert** button.

   A second **Item** element displays in the **Structure View**.

8. With the insertion point still to the right of the second **Item** element, in the **Element Catalog**, select **Para** and click **Insert**.

9. In the **Para** element, type: `Modem`

10. In the **Structure View**, click after the second **Item** element on the line descending from the **List** element.

11. In the **Element Catalog**, select **Item** and click the **Insert** button.

    A third **Item** element displays in **Structure View**.

12. In the **Para** element, type: `Transmission mode`

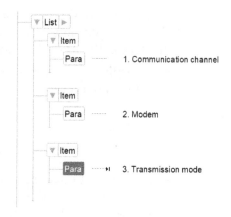

13. Collapse the Transmission Components **Section** element.

    All child elements are hidden under the collapsed **Section** element.

14. Select **File > Save** from the main menu.

Automatic insertion of child elements

Now that you have seen how structure creates more detail than unstructured systems require, it's time to see how we can use that to our advantage.

Elements can be defined so that when inserted, they automatically insert child elements. For example, when a **List** element is inserted, FrameMaker can automatically insert the **Item** and **Para** element required for a valid **List**.

Exercise 5:   Auto-inserting child elements

In this exercise, you will turn on the automatic insertion of child elements option. You will then insert several parent elements and see their child elements automatically inserted.

1. Select **Element > New Element Options** from the main menu.

   The **New Element Options** dialog box displays.

2. In the **Initial Structure** section, select (turn on) the **Allow Automatic Insertion of Children** check box.

3. Click the **Set** button.

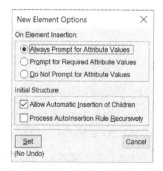

4. In the **Structure View**, click on the line below the collapsed Transmission Components **Section** element.

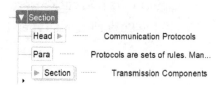

5. In the **Element Catalog**, select **Section** and click the **Insert** button.

    This time a **Head** element is automatically inserted as a child of **Section**, and your cursor is in the position to start typing text into the **Head** element.

6. In the **Head** element, type:
    ```
    Local Area Networks
    ```

7. In **Structure View**, click below the **Head** element.

8. In the **Element Catalog**, select **Para** and click the **Insert** button.

    The **Para** element displays in the **Structure View**.

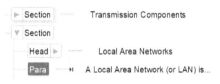

9. In the **Para** element, type:

    ```
    A Local Area Network (or LAN) is a set of microcomputers that
    communicate with each other through some physical media (such as
    coaxial cable).
    ```

10. In the **Structure View**, click below the **Para** element and insert another **Para** element.

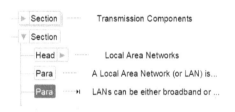

11. In the **Para** element, type:

    ```
    LANs can be either broadband or
    baseband. Most LANs are baseband LANs,
    using only one channel on the cable to
    support digital transmission.
    ```

12. In the **Structure View**, click below the **Para** element you just added and insert a **Section** element.

    The **Head** element is automatically inserted.

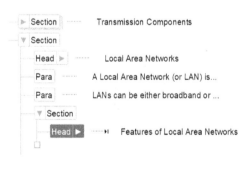

13. In the **Head** element, type: `Features of Local Area Networks`

14. In the **Structure View**, click below the **Head** element and insert a **Para** element.

    The **Para** element displays in the **Structure View**.

15. In the **Para** element, type:

    ```
    There are many benefits of a LAN. They include:
    ```

16. In the **Structure View**, click below the **Para** element.

17. Select the **List** element from the **Element Catalog** and click the **Insert** button.

    If the **Attributes for New Element** dialog displays, click the **Insert Element** button.

The **List** element, the **List** element's first **Item** element, and the **Item** element's first child **Para** element are automatically inserted.

18. In the **Para** element, type:
    ```
    Shared data and hardware
    ```

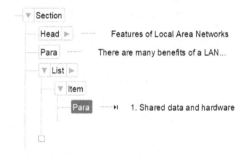

19. In the **Structure View**, use the image to the right to add the following text in the list by inserting **Item** elements.

    FrameMaker will automatically insert the **Para** elements for you.

Features of Local Area Networks

There are many benefits of a LAN. They include:

1. Shared data and hardware
2. More efficient use of hardware
3. E-mail capabilities
4. High-speed data transfer
5. Distributed processing
6. Better control over standard applications

20. Collapse the **Section** ("Features of Local Area Networks") element.

    The **List** element and all Item and **Para** descendant elements are hidden under the **Section** element.

21. Select **File > Save** from the main menu.

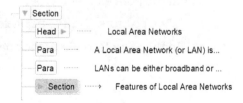

Correcting invalid elements

Whenever an element does not conform to the elements definitions of the document, the **Structure View** often identifies the error for you. Three types of element errors are visible in the structure view; a missing element, a misplaced element, and a collapsed element containing an error will all create red structure in the structure view.

In the **Structure View**, these elements are represented with special symbols.

- A square appears if a required element is missing. The **Element Catalog** displays the valid elements which can be inserted, and they are indicated with the check mark to the left of the element's name.

  This example also shows a collapsed **Section** element that contains an error.

- A vertical, dashed line appears from the location of the misplaced element.

  Move the invalid element to a new position or insert elements around the element to correct the error.

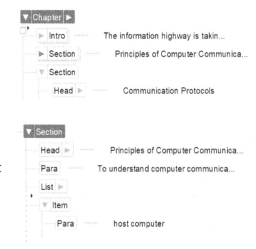

Importing Structured Content

You can import both structured and unstructured content using the **File>Import>File** command. The element definitions of the two documents do not have to be identical. However, when the structures differ, the imported content may be invalid and require correction. After importing this flow, you'll be able to manipulate the content as needed.

Both structured and unstructured content can also be copied and pasted between open FrameMaker documents.

 Exercise 6: Importing structured text

In this exercise, you will import structured text and specify its format.

1. In the **Structure View**, click below the collapsed "Features of Local Area Networks" **Section** element.

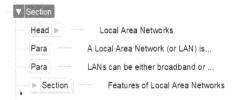

2. Select **File > Import > File** from the main menu.

   The **Import** dialog box displays.

3. If needed, navigate to the `AuthClass2020` directory.

4. Select the **Copy Into Document** option at the bottom of the dialog.

5. Select the `StructContentImport.fm` file.

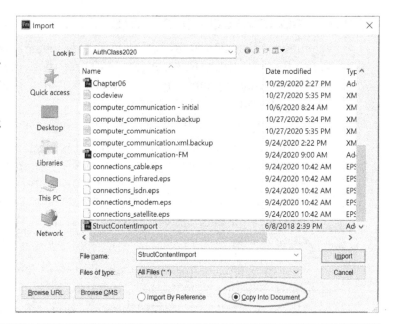

FrameMaker can import text and graphics by reference (where a link is maintained) or by copying directly into the document. Importing by reference will not allow you to modify the content from within this document.

6. Click the **Import** button.

   The **Import Text Flow by Copy** dialog displays.

7. If not already on, select (turn on) the **Body Page Flow** radio button.

   The text to be imported is located in a body page text flow in `StructContentImport`, not in a reference page flow.

8. If not already selected, from the **Body Page Flow** drop down menu, select **A (Main Flow)**.

9. If not already on, select (turn on) the **Reformat Using Current Document's Catalogs** radio button.

   This helps format content based upon formatting definitions stored in the receiving document.

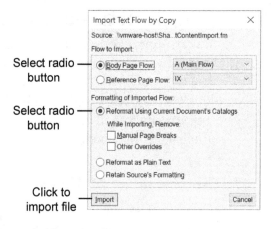

10. Click the **Import** button.

    The text and structure from `StructContentImport.fm` are imported at your insertion point and formatted using your document's formatting. An invalid element (NoName) appears in the **Structure View**, because the documents' structures are not identical.

    You will correct the invalid structure in the next exercise.

11. Select **File > Save** from the main menu.

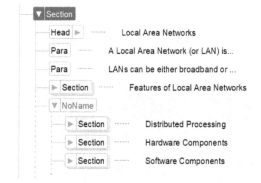

Moving Elements

You can move an element by dragging its bubble in the **Structure View**. If the element has any children, they will move too. You can also move an element by cutting and pasting the element to a new location. It is generally easier to move an element a short distance by dragging, and to move a long distance by cutting and pasting.

As you drag an element, an arrow will connect the element to the parent element it is being dragged through. If the line and bubble are red, the element is not valid at the current location.

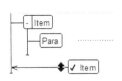

When the element is valid at the current position, the line and bubble will turn black, and a check mark appears inside the bubble.

Exercise 7:   Moving and unwrapping elements

In this exercise, you will correct the structure by moving and unwrapping.

There is often more than one way to fix an invalid structure.

1. In the **Structure View**, select the collapsed "Distributed Processing" **Section** element just imported.

2. Drag the **Section** element upward until it is just above the **NoName** element.

   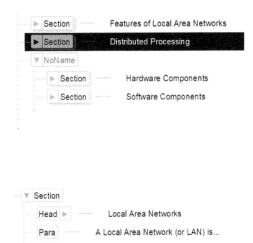

   An arrow connects the **Section** to its new parent as you drag. A check mark appears inside the bubble, indicating that the **Section** element is valid in this position.

   Instead of moving the second and third **Section** elements, you will just unwrap the **No Name** element.

3. In the **Structure View**, select the **NoName** element.

4. Select **Element > Unwrap** from the main menu.

   The **NoName** element disappears, and the second **Section** (Hardware Components) and third **Section** (Software Components) elements appear as siblings to the first **Section** (Distributed Processing) element you moved up earlier.

Exercise 8:   More moving by dragging

In this exercise, you will rearrange the elements of a list.

1. In the structure view, locate and expand the "Features of Local Area Networks" **Section** element.

2. Locate the **List** element under the **Section** element.

3. Shift-click the triangle on the right side of an **Item** to collapse the current element and its siblings.

4. By dragging and moving the **Item** elements in the **List** element, alphabetize the **Item** elements. For example, move Item 6 to Item 1 position, since Item 6 starts with a "B".

5. Select **File > Save** from the main menu.

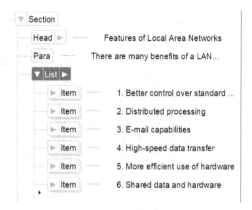

> You can't drag more than one element at a time in the structure view. Use Cut/Paste to move a selection of elements.

Exercise 9:   Moving by cutting and pasting

In this exercise, you will move an entire **Section** element by cutting and pasting in the **Structure View**.

1. In the **Structure View**, select the collapsed "Software Components" **Section** element.

2. Select **Edit > Cut** from the main menu.

   The **Section** element and its descendants are cut from the document window and pasted to the clipboard.

3. In the **Structure View**, click above the "Hardware Components" **Section** element.

4. Select **Edit > Paste** from the main menu.

   The "Software Components" **Section** element and its descendants are pasted at the insertion point.

5. Select **File > Save** from the main menu.

Wrapping and Unwrapping Elements

You can add structure to text and graphics, which have already been entered into a document, by *wrapping* an element around the contents. Wrapping is also used for adding structure to an unstructured document.

When you wrap an element, a pair of element boundaries appears around the contents in the document window, and a new bubble appears in the **Structure View**.

Unwrapping an element deletes the *element* from the structure but leaves its *contents* in the document.

Exercise 10: Wrapping and unwrapping text

In this exercise, you will wrap text into the element **Term** and unwrap other elements that no longer need structuring.

1. On page 1 in the document window, locate the paragraph following the heading "Host Computer."

    [[Host Computer]   [This is the computer where centralized data is stored, where processing can be done, and from where information is transmitted. Mainframe host computers usually use a piece of hardware called a front-end processor to manage the computer communications of the network that the host computer is a part of.

2. In the **Para** element, select the text "front-end processor".

3. In the **Element Catalog**, select **Term** and click the **Wrap** ([ ])button.

    Because you previously set **New Element Options** to **Always Prompt for Attribute Values**, the **Attributes for New Element** dialog box displays. In a future exercise you will choose **Prompt for Required Attribute Values** to speed things up.

4. Click the **Wrap Element** button.

    The text "front-end processor" is wrapped in the **Term** element.

5. Locate the **Term** containing the phrase "Interneters" in the first **Para** of your document.

6. Select **Element > Unwrap** from the main menu.

    The text is now unwrapped and becomes part of the parent **Para** element.

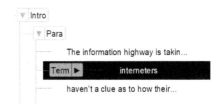

7. Select **File > Save** from the main menu.

Formatting phrases

A little creativity can help you save time when wrapping phrases in structured elements.

 Exercise 11: Use Find/Change to wrap common phrases

In this exercise you will copy an element containing a phrase to the clipboard and then replace all instances of the phrase within your document.

1. Select the **Term** containing the phrase "front-end processor" in the **Intro** element.

2. Use **Edit>Copy** to place the element and its content on the clipboard.

3. Place your cursor after the term you just copied.

4. Navigate to the **Find/Change (Ctrl+F)** panel and search for the phrase "front-end processor" as show here.

5. Set the **Change** option to **By Pasting**.

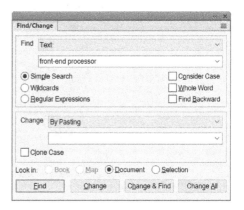

6. Select the **Find** button to find the next instance of "front-end processor" in your document.

> [The software involved at this level includes the operating system software for the host computer, which includes the communications software the host uses (often called a NCP, network control program) in the **front-end processor**.]]

7. Press the **Change** button to replace the phrase with an element containing the phrase.

8. Press the **Find** button again.

    The first instance of the term is selected, but *not* the element boundaries. For this reason you need to move carefully when using **Find/Replace** to avoid inadvertently creating invalid structure.

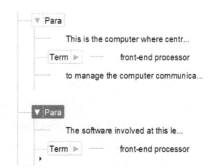

Merging and Splitting Elements

The **Merge** command merges all of the elements you select into the first element in the selection.

You can also split an element into two separate elements of the same type and same level. For example, you may decide that a **Para** needs to be divided into two **Para** elements.

 Exercise 12: Merging elements

In this exercise, you will use the **Merge** command to merge two **Para** elements into one.

1. In the document window, the two paragraphs in the "Distributed Processing" section near the end of your document as shown.

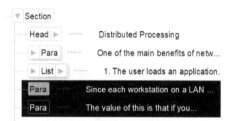

2. Select **Element > Merge** from the main menu.

   The second **Para** element is merged into the first.

3. Select **File > Save** from the main menu.

[Since each workstation on a LAN operates in this manner, the total computer power of the network is distributed amongst all the microprocessors in each microcomputer.The value of this is that if you run out of capacity in a mainframe environment you must incur a huge charge to upgrade, whereas in a LAN environment, you can often simply add more microcomputers to the network.]]

 Exercise 13: Splitting an element

In this exercise, you will use the **Split** command to divide a **Para** element within an **Item** element into two **Para** elements.

1. In the document window, locate the **List** element in the "Distributed Processing" **Section** and place the insertion point as shown

   1. [[[The user loads an application on his or her workstations. The application may be automatically loaded from the file server or may exist locally. As the application is running, data is retrieved from the file server, where it resides.]]

2. Select **Element > Split** from the main menu.

   The **Para** element is divided into two. The second **Para** element is formatted differently, as it is not the first **Para** in an **Item**.

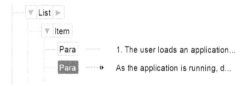

3. Select **File > Save** from the main menu.

Exercise 14: Changing an element

In this exercise, you will change a **Para** element into a **Note** element.

1. In the **Structure View**, locate the "Software Components" **Section** element.

2. Select the first paragraph after the **List** element.

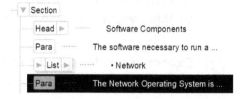

3. In the **Element Catalog**, select **Note** and click the **Change** button.

The **Note** element is changed into a **Para** element, which results in changes in ruling and a Note: prefix.

4. Select **File > Save** from the main menu, and then select **File > Close**.

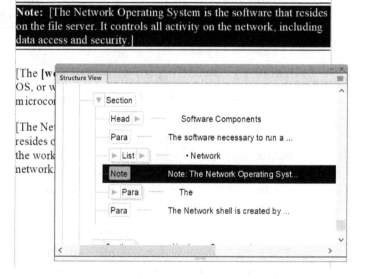

Chapter 6: Attributes

Introduction

In this module, you will work with attributes. You will set the way attributes are inserted and displayed in a structured document. You will also use the Attributes panel to insert attribute values for new elements and change attributes of existing elements.

Module Objectives

In this module, you will learn how to:

- Change the attribute display.
- Change prompting for attributes on element insertion.
- Provide attribute values for new elements.
- Modify attribute values of existing elements.
- Recognize invalid attributes and correct them.

Working with Attributes

FrameMaker provides *attributes* to supply additional information about an element. For example, the template designer could use an attribute called *Version* for its *Chapter* element to allow the user to specify the chapter's revision status. A common use of attributes is to specify formatting information.

The following examples show how attributes might be used in a structured document:

- A Security attribute in a highest-level element might specify the level of classification for a document's contents, such as **Security=Unclassified**.
- An Author attribute in a Chapter element might specify the author of the document, such as **Author=Fred**.
- A Type attribute in a List element might specify the list style, such as **Type=Bulleted**.

All attributes have:

- An attribute name.
- A definition of required, for validity or optional.
- An attribute type, such as String, Integer, Real, or Choice.

Attributes can have:

- A default value (optional attributes only).
- A range of valid values (numeric attributes only).
- A definition of Read-Only (not modifiable, software provides value).

Changing attribute display

Element attributes can be viewed directly in the **Structure View**. The **Attribute Display** command controls **Structure View** attribute display options.

Depending on which setting you choose, the **Structure View** displays:

- Required attributes and any optional attributes for which a value has been given.
- All attributes.
- No attributes.

Exercise 1:   Displaying attributes

In this exercise, you will practice displaying the attributes in your document.

1. From the `AuthClass2020` directory, open `Chapter06.fm`.

   a. Select **File > Open** from the main menu.

      The **Open** dialog box displays.

   b. If necessary, change to the `AuthClass2020` directory.

   c. Double-click `Chapter06.fm`.

      The document displays in the document window.

2. If not already open, open the **Structure View**.

3. Select **View > Attribute Display Options** from the main menu.

   The **Attribute Display Options** dialog box displays.

4. Select the **No Attributes** radio button.

5. Click the **Set** button.

   In the **Structure View**, notice the triangle symbols on the right side of the **Chapter**, **Head**, and other elements, indicating the presence of attributes.

6. In the **Structure View**, click the right-facing arrow symbol (▶) on the right side of the **Chapter** element. You may notice slightly different values and behavior for the **Chapter** attributes than you saw in previous sections.

   The first click on the right-facing arrow symbol (▶) displays required attributes, and any optional attributes that have specified values.

7. Click the right-facing arrow symbol (▶) on the right side of the **Chapter** element again to display all attributes associated with the **Chapter** element.

   The second click displays any remaining attributes, if there are attributes that were not displayed with the first click.

8. Click the downward-facing arrow symbol (▼) on the right side of the **Chapter** element to hide the attributes.

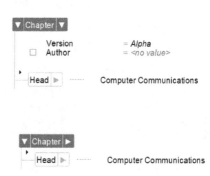

Choosing attribute values

Some attributes are editable by the author. You supply values for these attributes in the **Attributes** panel.

For a selected attribute, FrameMaker displays:

- Current attribute **Value**, if any.
- Whether a value is **Required** for validity, or **Optional**.
- **Attribute Type**, such as **String**, **Integer**, **Real**, or **Choice**.
- Any default value (optional attributes only) to be used if a value is not specified.
- Any range of values (numeric attributes only).
- Whether the attribute is **Read-Only** (not modifiable by the author).

If you try to enter a value that is not valid, FrameMaker will reject the value and display an alert.

The Attribute Type can be defined as:

Type:	Explanation:
String	Arbitrary text string
Strings	One or more arbitrary text strings
Integer	Single whole number; can be signed
Integers	One or more integers, can be signed
Real	Real number; can be signed
Reals	One or more real numbers; can be signed
Choice	Value from a list of choices
UniqueId	String that uniquely identifies the element
IDReference	Reference to a UniqueID attribute
IDReferences	One or more references to a UniqueID attribute

Exercise 2: Changing a string value

In this exercise, you will change the value of the **Chapter** element's **Author** attribute to your name.

1. If the **Attributes** panel isn't visible, double-click on one of the attributes on the **Chapter** element. You may need to expand the **Chapter** attributes before you can double-click.

   The **Attributes** panel displays the **Chapter** element's attributes.

2. In the **Attribute Name** list, select **Author**.

3. If necessary, click on the triangle to the right of the **Chapter** bubble to view both the **Author** and **Version** attributes in the **Structure View**.

   The **Author** attribute value is missing, resulting in the red box next to **Author** in the **Structure View**.

4. In the **Attributes** panel, place your cursor in the **Value** field and type in your name, and press **Tab** or **Enter**.

   In the **Structure View**, the **Author** attribute now contains your name.

5. Select **File > Save** from the main menu.

Exercise 3: Changing a choice attribute

In this exercise, you will change the value for the **Version** attribute to **Final**.

1. In the **Attributes** panel, select **Version** in the **Attribute Name** scroll list.

   The attribute value for **Version** is blank in the **Attribute Value** scroll list. Because **Alpha** is defined as the default value, that's what is displayed in the **Structure View**.

2. Click the arrow in the **Value** field to display the available choices, and select **Final**.

In the **Structure View**, the **Version** attribute field displays the value **Final**.

Note also that since there is now an explicit value for **Version**, the value is no longer displayed in italic.

3. Select **File > Save** from the main menu.

Inserting New Elements and Attributes

When new elements are added, you can control how FrameMaker prompts for required or optional attribute values in the **New Element Options** dialog box. You may find that prompting only for required attributes is a balanced choice for this setting.

 Exercise 4:   Prompting for attribute values

In this exercise, you will choose an alternate setting for prompting of attribute values when inserting new elements.

1. Select **Element > New Element Options** from the main menu.

   The **New Element Options** dialog box displays.

2. Select the **Prompt for Required Attribute Values** choice.

3. Click the **Set** button.

4. In the **Structure View**, navigate to and expand the "Local Area Networks" **Section** element.

5. In the **Structure View**, place the insertion point below the first **Para** element in the expanded **Section**.

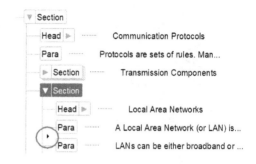

6. Insert a **List** element from the **Element Catalog**.

   Because you are now prompting for only required attributes, the **Attributes for New Element** dialog doesn't display.

   The **Item** and **Para** elements are automatically inserted, as long as your new element options are still set to allow automatic insertion of children from an earlier exercise.

7. Select the new **List** element in the structure view and set the **Type** attribute to **Bullet** in the **Attributes** panel.

8. Type **Ethernet cable** in the **Para** element of your new list.

9. Fill out the remainder of your list by following the accompanying image.

10. Select **File > Save** from the main menu.

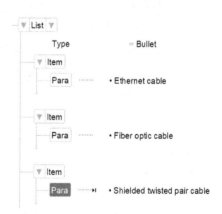

Recognizing and Correcting Attributes with Errors

Attributes errors can occur because:

- A required value is missing.

  This error is identified with a square next to the attribute.

- A provided value is of the wrong type, outside the specified range, or not one of the possible choices

  For example, for a system with a **Version** attribute not allowing a value of **Completed**, if you import a chapter with a type of **Completed**, you would see an error (**x**) next to the **Version** attribute. The attribute would remain black, but the x and the value would be displayed in red.

- The **Attribute Name**, itself, is undefined in this document.

  For example, if you import structure with different attributes than your system allows, you will see an error. The entire undefined attribute and its value will display in red.

 Exercise 5:   Deleting a required attribute value

In this exercise, you will delete the value of the Author attribute on the Chapter element.

1. Select the **Chapter** element in the **Structure View**.

2. In the **Attributes** panel, select the current **Author** attribute value, which you set earlier to your name.

3. Clear the value by deleting the text and pressing **Tab** or **Enter**.

   Because the **Author** attribute is required, you are prompted with a confirmation dialog box.

4. Look back at the structure view, and confirm that the phrase "<no value>" displays for the **Author** attribute.

If **Author** had been an optional attribute with a default value, the default value would have displayed in italics, because it is a default value, not an actual specified value.

5. Select **File > Save** from the main menu, and then select **File > Close**.

▼ Chapter ▼

　　　Version　　　　= Final
☐　Author　　　　= *<no value>*

Chapter 7: Validation

Introduction

In this module, you will use the validation command to find and fix invalid element structure.

Module Objectives

In this module, you will learn how to:

- Use the **Element Validation** dialog box.
- Specify the scope of validation.
- Correct invalid structure.
- Use **Ignore Missing Elements** and **Ignore Missing Attribute Values** effectively.
- Allow an invalid element as a special case.

Validating a Document's Structure

Many authoring environments require that the document or book's structure be valid at the completion of a project. For example, a consumer electronics company may save content as XML to gain efficiency with translation/localization efforts. Invalid content would limit automated, or machine translation of the content. This would result in increased handwork and cost. Other potential consequences might be missing text, incorrect formatting, or other document or book corruption.

In FrameMaker, valid structure is required to save XML formats (XML, DITA, DITAMAP, etc.) but not required to share native (.fm and .book) documents with other FrameMaker authors.

Before documents are completed and fully valid, they may go through many iterations of development. All FrameMaker features work with valid and invalid documents.

All documents, however, should be fully valid before delivering a project.

In addition to using the **Structure View** to find errors, you can have FrameMaker *validate* a document, and identify misplaced and missing elements and attribute values. You can validate an entire document, the current flow, or just the current element.

When FrameMaker validates a document against the content model, it searches for elements and attributes that do not match their rules in the **Element Catalog**. Validation errors may occur when an element, or attribute value, is missing, misplaced, or contains illegal values.

When the validation command locates an error, it describes the error in the **Element Validation** dialog box. Once you know where the structural errors are in a document, you can use the **Element Validation** panel, **Element Catalog**, **Document View**, **Attributes** panel, and **Structure View** to correct them.

See the following page for some of the more common validation errors you'll find.

Validation Error:	Explanation:
Current flow is unstructured	The current flow contains no elements.
Element is undefined	The element is not defined in the document. You may have copied this element from another document.
Missing element before *tag*	At least one required element is missing before the specified element.
More contents required at end	At least one more child element is required at the end of the current element.
No current element	There is no insertion point or selection. (This message appears when the scope is set to Current Element.)
No current flow	There is no insertion point or selection. (This message appears when the scope is set to Current Flow.)
Not highest-level element	The element is not permitted at the highest level in the document.
<TEXT> not permitted in this element	The element contains text, but text is not allowed.
<TEXT> not valid at this position	The element may allowed to have contain text, but not here. Wrapping text in another container element may resolve this.
The *name* **attribute refers to an undefined ID value**	The attribute is an IDReference and refers to a UniqueID value that doesn't exist in the document (or in the book, if you're validating a book).
The *name* **attribute is undefined for this element**	The definition of this element does not include an attribute with the specified label. This may occur after updates to your content model.
This element should be a *type*	The element is the wrong type, where *type* can be *graphic, cross-reference, equation, marker,* or *system variable.* For example, a cross-reference element might consist of text instead of a cross-reference.
Value must be a *type* **for** *name* **attribute**	The attribute value is the wrong type for the attribute.
Value for *name* **attribute must be in the range from** *n* **to** *n*	The attribute's numeric value is out of the specified range.
Value for *name* **attribute is not one of the allowed choices**	The attribute's value must match a value from the pop-up menu of valid choices.
Value for *name* **attribute must be unique**	A UniqueID value must be unique for all elements in the document or book.
Value required for *name* **attribute**	An attribute value is required but has not been supplied. The attribute's value cannot be left blank.
tag **excluded in this element**	The *tag* element is not allowed anywhere in the parent element in its current context.
tag **not permitted in this element**	The *tag* element is not allowed anywhere in the parent element.
tag **not valid at this position**	The element is allowed in the parent element, but not at the current location.

Exercise 1:   Setting up for validation

In this exercise, you will use the **Element Validation** dialog box to find and correct the structural errors in your document.

1. From the `Class` directory, open `mod07.fm`.

2. Display the following structure components, if not already visible:

    · Structure View

    · Element Catalog

    · Attributes

    · Element Validation (**Structure>Validate**)

3. If necessary, show element boundaries using the **View>Element Boundaries** menu item.

4. In the **Elements** panel options (⚙), set **Show These Elements:** to **Valid Elements for Working Start to Finish**, and set **Inclusions:** to **List after Other Valid Elements**.

    These options will help you understand your most likely solutions while validating content.

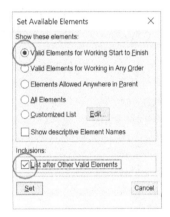

5. In the **Structure View**, place the insertion point under the **Chapter** element at the beginning of the document.

    Validation moves forward from the insertion point.

6. In the **Element Validation** dialog box, select the **Entire Document** radio button, if necessary, and deselect the **Ignore Missing Elements** and **Ignore Missing Attribute Values** check boxes.

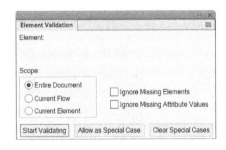

Exercise 2:   Validating basic errors

In this exercise you will practice identifying the element containing the validation error, and assessing your options for correcting the error.

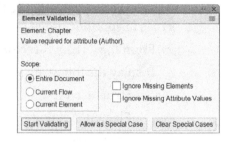

1. Click the **Start Validating** button.

   The upper-left corner of the **Element Validation** panel identifies the first error as a missing attribute on the **Chapter** element.

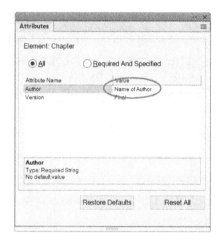

2. Correct the missing author attribute by typing your name into the **Author** attribute field.

   Press either the **Enter** or **Tab** key to accept the attribute change.

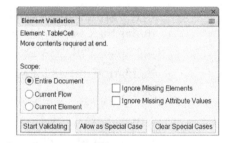

3. Select the **Start Validating** button to continue validating.

   The **Element Validation** panel describes the error as something missing at the end of the table cell.

   However, in looking at the cell above, you'll find that the **Xref** element should be wrapped in a **Para** element.

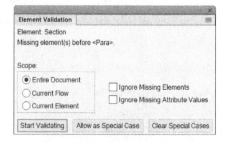

4. Select the **Start Validating** button to continue validating.

   The **Element Validation** panel identifies the error as an element missing within the **Section** element.

   In the **Structure View**, the insertion point displays in the **Section** element at the point of the invalid structure. The red square indicates that an element is missing.

To view the point at which the error occurs, you may need to expand the **Section** element.

The **Element Catalog** indicates that a **Head** element would be valid at the insertion point.

However, if you look closely, you'll find that the heading content you need, *LAN Components*, is already in the document. It's just been placed incorrectly inside a **Para** element, rather than a **Head** element.

5. To fix the incorrect structure, select the **Para** element containing the **LAN Components** text in the **Structure View**.

6. In the **Element Catalog**, select **Head** and then click the **Change** (🖉) button.

The **Para** element changes to a **Head** element, and the invalid structure indicators disappear.

The formatting also improves, with the proper first-level heading characteristics.

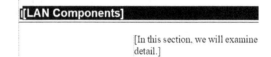

Exercise 3:   Correcting Illegal attribute values

If your content model changes, or you receive content from other organizations, you may occasionally find elements and attributes that are not part of your allowable content model.

As with other types of validation errors, use the indicators in your pods and windows to determine the most logical option.

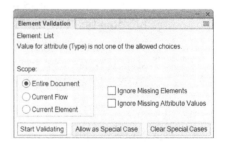

1. In the **Element Validation** dialog box, click the **Start Validating** button.

The validation process continues from the insertion point.

The **Element Validation** dialog box identifies the next error as part of a **List** element; "Value for attribute (Type) is not one of the allowed choices".

In this case, the **Type** attribute for **List** elements does not permit **Alpha**, the current value for the attribute.

If needed, expand the **Section** element and expand the attributes on the **List** element to get a better sense of what is causing the error.

2. To fix the problem, set the **Type** attribute to **Bullet** within the **Attributes** panel.

While the **Number** and **EmDash** attributes are also valid choices, the **Number** value implies an order of operation, while the **EmDash** might be better used for a second-level unordered list.

3. Select **File > Save** from the main menu.

Exercise 4:   Correcting by nudging

In this exercise, you'll find a paragraph that's been inadvertently placed inside a heading element.

By moving the improperly placed content, you will correct two errors simultaneously, using a technique known as *nudging*.

4. In the **Element Validation** dialog box, click the **Start Validating** button.

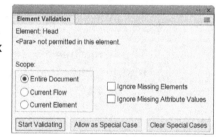

The upper-left corner of the **Element Validation** dialog box identifies the next error as occurring within a **Head** element. Specifically, the error is **<Para> not permitted in this element**.

Expand the **Section** element if needed to get a better sense of the problem.

Notice that the **Head** element contains not only heading text but also an invalid **Para** child element.

The **Para** element needs to be promoted in the structure (moved to the left) so that it is a sibling to the **Head** element, rather than a child.

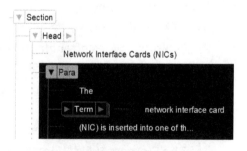

5. Move the cursor over the selected **Para** element.

6. Hold down the mouse button and drag the bubble slightly (about the width of one character, or about 3 screen pixels) to the left.

As you drag, the cursor on the **Para** element bubble changes to a left arrow.

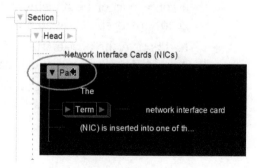

If your left-facing arrow instead becomes an up and down arrow, you've drug too far to the left. Release your mouse and repeat the process, this time dragging more slowly.

It may take some practice, but when you have large chunks of content, this is an excellent way to rearrange content without using cut/paste, and without having to noodle with collapsing structure in order to view both the original and destination locations in the structure view simultaneously.

7. As soon as you see the left arrow on the **Para** element, release the mouse button.

    The element jumps into place as a sibling of the **Head** element.

    Similarly, an element can be demoted to become a child of the sibling immediately preceding it by dragging the bubble slightly (about the width of one character) to the right. As you drag, the pointer on the bubble changes to a right arrow.

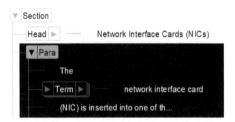

Exercise 5:   Correcting other nesting problems

In this example you'll find valid structure that has been wrapped in an unneeded element.

While the problem may not be immediately obvious, when looking at complex portions of structure you will benefit from comparing the invalid structure to other similar pieces of valid structure.

1. Click the **Start Validating** button.

    The upper-left corner of the **Element Validation** dialog box identifies the next error as a **List** element; "**<Para> not permitted in this element**".

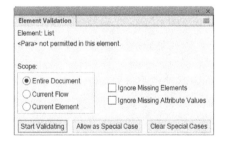

The **Item** element has been incorrectly wrapped in a **Para** element.

2. To remove the unneeded Para element, select **Element > Unwrap** from the main menu.

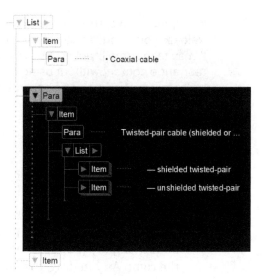

The **Item** element is unwrapped from the **Para** element.

3. Select **File > Save** from the main menu.

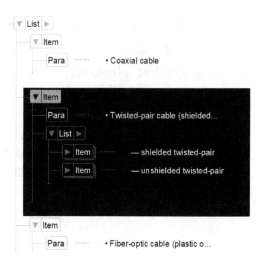

Special Cases for Elements and Attributes

The validation command will stop at every invalid element or attribute in a document or flow. Occasionally, an invalid or misplaced element or attribute cannot be corrected because:

- You do not yet know how to make the correction.
- The invalid element or attribute will become valid when you add or modify structure at a later time.

To have the validation command pass over these problems until a later time when they will be corrected, use the **Allow as Special Case** option in the **Element Validation** dialog box. FrameMaker will skip over these special cases until you clear them with the **Clear Special Cases** option.

 Exercise 6:   Allowing a special case

In this exercise, you will allow a missing attribute value as a special case.

1. Select the **Chapter** element in the **Structure View**.
2. In the **Attributes** panel, delete the value of the **Author** attribute.
3. If necessary, in the **Element Validation** dialog box, deselect the **Ignore Missing Attribute Values** check box.
4. In the **Element Validation** dialog box, click the **Start Validating** button.

    The upper-left corner of the **Element Validation** dialog box identifies the element containing the error as the **Chapter** element.
    The error is **Value required for attribute (Author)**.

    If you're unsure of who will be listed as the final author of this content, you might choose to bypass this validation error and allow this as a special case.

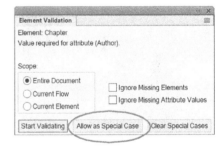

5. Click the **Allow As Special Case** button.
6. In the **Element Validation** dialog box, click the **Start Validating** button.

    The **Element Validation** dialog box indicates the "**Document is valid**".

    Select **File > Save** from the main menu.

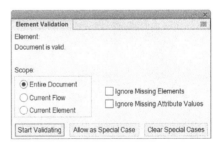

Chapter 8: New Documents and Structure Shortcuts

Introduction

In this module, you will explore options for creating a new structured document into which you can place your content.

You will also practice inserting elements using keyboard shortcuts.

Module Objectives

- Create a new structured document with **Save As**.
- Create a new structured document by importing formats and element definitions.
- Use keyboard shortcuts to insert and edit elements.

Creating Structured Documents

FrameMaker provides a number of ways to create new structured documents, including:

- By importing element and formats definitions from a structured template.
- By using the **Save As** command while in a structured template or document.

After creating a new document containing an element catalog and other FrameMaker formatting options, you add structure to a new document by inserting elements.

You can enter all of the proper elements as you go along, or you can work more loosely, concentrating on content rather than on structure, later validating the document to correct errors.

You can also add structure to an existing, unstructured document by wrapping its contents in elements.

There are two parts to the formatting that you'll see in a structured document:

- The "classic" FrameMaker formatting options, brought into another document using the **Import Formats** command.
- The **Element Catalog**, which is stored in a document called the **EDD**, or **Element Definition Document**. You import or update these definitions into another FrameMaker document using the **Import Element Definitions** command.

Exercise 1:   Creating a new structured document by importing elements and formats

In the following exercise you will create a new, unstructured document and import formats and element definitions from `Chapter08.fm`, which you will use as your structured template.

1. From the `AuthClass2020` directory, open `Chapter08.fm`.

   Note that `Chapter08.fm` does not contain content. You'll use this file only for importing of formats.

2. Ensure that both the **Borders** and the **Element Boundaries** are visible.

3. If not already open, open the **Structure View** and the **Element Catalog**.

   Although the document view and structure view are blank, notice that (depending on your Element Catalog options) when you place your cursor in the body page text box there are one or more elements visible in the **Element Catalog**.

4. Create a **New Portrait** document.

   a. Select **File > New > Document** from the main menu.

      The **New** dialog box displays.

   b. Click the **Portrait** button at the top of the dialog.

   A new FrameMaker document, `Untitled1.fm`, displays. Because this document has no structure model associated with it, the document view, the **Structure View**, and the **Element Catalog** in this document are all empty.

5. Use the **Save As** dialog box to save the document in the `AuthClass2020` directory with the new filename `AuthoringPractice.fm`.

6. Import all formats from `Chapter08.fm` into `AuthoringPractice.fm`.

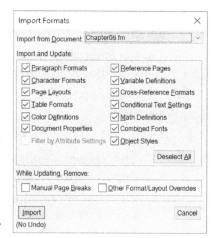

   a. If necessary, make `AuthoringPractice.fm` the active document in FrameMaker.

   b. Select **File > Import > Formats** from the main menu.

      The **Import Formats** dialog box displays.

   c. From the **Import from Document** drop-down menu, select `Chapter08.fm`.

   d. In the **Import and Update** area, select all (enable checkmarks) of the format check boxes.

   e. Click the **Import** button.

      Paragraph, character, table, page layout and other formats are imported into `AuthoringPractice.fm`.

7. Show tags for **All Elements**.

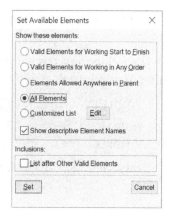

   a. Select **Element > Set Available Elements** from the main menu.

      The **Set Available Elements** dialog box displays.

   b. Select (turn on) the **All Elements** radio button.

c. Click the **Set** button.

While you did import formatting information, the **Element Catalog** is still empty because you haven't yet imported a content model (your element definitions) into the new document.

8. Import element definitions from Chapter08.fm into AuthoringPractice.fm.

   a. Select **File > Import > Element Definitions** from the main menu.

   The **Import Element Definitions** dialog box displays.

   b. From the **Import from Document** drop-down menu, select Chapter08.fm.

   c. Click the **Import** button.

   The **Element Catalog** now displays all of the elements imported from Chapter08.fm.

9. Show tags for **Valid Elements for Working Start to Finish**.

   a. Select **Element > Set Available Elements** from the main menu.

   The **Set Available Elements** dialog box displays.

   b. Select (turn on) the **Valid Elements for Working Start to Finish** radio button.

   c. Select (turn on) the **Inclusions: List after Other Valid Elements** option.

   d. Click the **Set** button.

The **Element Catalog** displays **Chapter** as the element valid at the highest level in the structure.

At this point, you could begin authoring your document using the document window, **Structure View**, and **Element Catalog** to guide you.

Instead, you will begin a structured document using the second method.

10. Select **File > Save** from the main menu, and then **File > Close**.

Exercise 2:   Creating a new structured document with Save As

In this exercise, you will use the **Save As** command to more rapidly create a new structured document that is the same as the one from the previous exercise.

1. Ensure that Chapter08.fm is the active FrameMaker document.

2. Use **File>Save As** to save Chapter08.fm in the AuthClass2020 directory with the new filename SaveAsPractice.fm.

   a. In Chapter08.fm, select **File > Save As** from the main menu.

The **Save Document** dialog box displays.

b. If necessary, change to the `AuthClass2020` directory.

c. In the **File name** field, delete the current file name and type: `SaveAsPractice`

d. Click the **Save** button.

At this point, your two new documents are basically the same and you could begin authoring in either `AuthoringPractice.fm` or `SaveAsPractice.fm` using the document window, **Structure View**, and **Element Catalog** to guide you.

3. Select **File > Save** from the main menu, and then **File > Close**.

In the next section you'll learn about some shortcuts that can speed your creation and editing of content.

Element Keyboard Shortcuts

FrameMaker provides many keyboard shortcuts when working with elements.

The following keyboard shortcuts can be used to select, insert, wrap, change, merge, and split elements:

Shortcut:	Action:
Esc h E	Select element containing the insertion point
Esc h N	Select next element
Esc h P	Select previous element
Esc h S	Select siblings of current element
Esc h e P	Select parent element of current element
Control-1	Insert an element
Control-2	Wrap a selection in an element
Control-3	Change an element
Esc E u	Unwrap an element
Esc E m	Merge element into first element
Esc E M	Merge element into last element
Esc E s	Split element
Esc e e	Repeat last insert, wrap, or change element command

Inserting elements

As long as your cursor is active in the document view you can insert an element at any time using the **Control+1** shortcut to bring up the Smart Insert for Elements dialog. In certain instances, pressing the **Enter** key can also be used to bring up this same dialog.

The effect of pressing the **Enter** key depends on the general rules of the element that contains the insertion point. When you press **Enter**, FrameMaker checks the current element's rule for one of the following conditions—*in the order given*—and inserts an element as described below:

Table 1:

Situation:	Response:
Repeating element	Enter key adds another sibling element of the same type.
One valid element	Enter key adds that element.
More than one valid element	Enter key highlights Tag area, prompting for element name. Type the name of element and press Enter key.
End of an element	If no more child elements are valid, Enter looks for valid elements in ancestors. If no valid elements, FrameMaker beeps.
None of above	Enter key causes FrameMaker to beep.

Exercise 3:   Inserting elements using shortcuts

In this exercise, you will insert **Section**, **Para**, and **Note** elements using the **Control+1** shortcut keys. This illustration shows the elements and text you will insert at the end of your sample document.

1. From the `AuthClass2020` directory, open `Chapter08b.fm`.

2. If not already open, open the **Structure View** and the **Element Catalog**.

3. Select **View > Borders** from the main menu, then **View > Text Symbols**, and **View > Element Boundaries**.

4. In the **Structure View**, place the insertion point at the end of the document, after the last **Section** element.

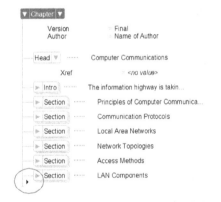

5. Press **Control+1** (Press and hold down the **Control** key, then press **1**).

   The **Smart Insert for Elements** dialog box displays at the insertion point in the **Structure View**, prompting you to type the name of the element that you want to insert. Note that the **Section** element displays in the list as a valid element.

6. Start to type: `Section`

FrameMaker filters available elements using the characters you type into the Smart Insert dialog.

7. As soon as **Section** is highlighted in the **Insert Element** dialog, press the **Enter** key.

   The **Section** element is inserted.
   A **Head** element is also automatically inserted.

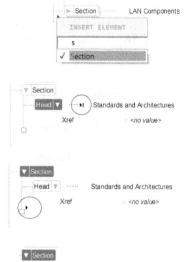

8. In the **Head** element, type:
   ```
   Standards and Architectures
   ```
   After typing, your insertion point is now at the end of the **Head** element.

9. Press the **right arrow key** once to move out of the **Head** element.

   The insertion point is now outside of the **Head** element but still inside the **Section** element.

10. Press **Control + 1**.

    The **Smart Insert for Elements** dialog box displays at the insertion point in the **Structure View**, prompting you to type the name of the element that you want to insert. Note that the **Para** element displays in the list as a valid element.

 Depending on the specific build of FrameMaker you have installed, inclusions may or may not display the check plus icons that you would expect in the **Element Catalog**.

11. Start to type: `Para`

    Para is highlighted in the **Search** field as a valid element.

12. Press the **Enter** key.

    The **Para** element is inserted.

13. In the **Para** element, type:

    ```
    Many different devices from different manufacturers comprise the
    basic components of a LAN. Each must be able to communicate with
    each other.
    ```

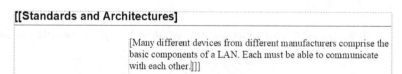

14. Press the **right arrow key**, once, to move out of the **Para** element.

15. Press **Control + 1**.

The **Insert Element** dialog box displays at the insertion point in the **Structure View**, prompting you to type the name of the element you want to insert. Note that the **Figure**, **List**, **Note**, **Para**, **Section**, and **Table** elements display in the **Element Catalog** as a valid elements.

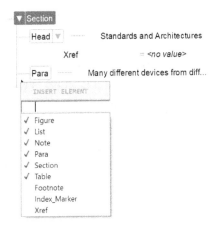

16. Start to type: `Para`

    Para is highlighted in the **Search** field as a valid element.

17. Press the **Enter** key.

    The **Para** element is inserted.

18. In the **Para** element, type:

    ```
    A network architecture can be broken into layers, with each layer
    responsible for a certain task. There are also protocols that
    define how layers communicate with each other.
    ```

19. Press the **Enter** key.

    Since the **Para** element is defined as a repeating element (same element more than once, consecutively), the **Para** element is inserted.

20. In the **Para** element, type:

    ```
    The layering of protocols to create
    network architectures is a basic
    principle of standards-based networking.
    ```

21. Press the **Enter** key.

    Another **Para** element is inserted.

22. In the **Para** element, type:

    ```
    Originally released in 1978, the OSI model describes a network
    architecture to connect dissimilar devices.
    ```

23. Press the **right arrow key** once to move out of the **Para** element.

24. Press **Control + 1**.

    The **Insert Element** dialog box displays at the insertion point in the **Structure View**, prompting you to type the name of the element you want to insert. Note that the **Figure**, **List**, **Note**, **Para**, **Section**, and **Table** elements display in the **Element Catalog** as a valid elements.

25. Start to type: `Note`

    Note is highlighted in the **Search** field as a valid element.

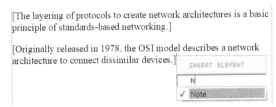

26. Press the **Enter** key.

    The **Note** element is inserted.

The **Note**: text appears automatically in the document. In this particular structure, you cannot directly enter text in a **Note** element. To enter text, you must first insert a **Para** element as a child of the **Note** element.

[Originally released in 1978, the OSI model describes a network architecture to connect dissimilar devices.]

Note: []]]

27. Press **Control + 1**.

    The **Insert Element** dialog box displays at the insertion point in the **Structure View**, prompting you to type the name of the element you want to insert. Note that **Para** displays in the **Element Catalog** as a valid element.

28. Start to type: `Para`

    Para is highlighted in the **Search** field as a valid element.

29. Press the **Enter** key.

    The **Para** element is inserted.

30. In the **Para** element, type:

    ```
    The development of the OSI
    model is an ongoing process.
    ```

[Originally released in 1978, the OSI model describes a network architecture to connect dissimilar devices.]

Note: [[The development of the OSI model is an ongoing process.]]]]

31. Select **File > Save** from the main menu.

Exercise 4:   Inserting elements using the Enter key

In this exercise, you will insert **Section**, **Para** and **Head** elements using the **Enter** key.

1. If needed, place your cursor at the end of the document structure.

2. Press the **Enter** key.

    The **Insert Element** dialog box displays at the insertion point in the **Structure View**, prompting you to type the name of the element you want to insert. Note that the **Section** element displays in the **Element Catalog** as a valid element.

3. Start to type: `Section`

    Section is highlighted in the **Search** field as a valid element.

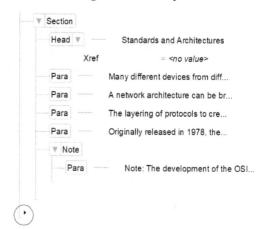

4. Press the **Enter** key.

    The **Section** element is inserted. A **Head** element is also automatically inserted.

5. In the **Head** element, type: `Network Interface Layers`

6. Press the **right arrow key**, once, to move out of the **Head** element.

7. Press the **Enter** key.

    The **Insert Element** dialog box displays at the insertion point in the **Structure View**, prompting you to type the name of the element you want to insert. Note that the **Para** element displays in the **Element Catalog** as a valid element.

8. Start to type: `Para`

    Para is highlighted in the **Search** field as a valid element.

9. Press the **Enter** key.

    The **Para** element is inserted.

10. In the **Para** element, type:

    ```
    The network interface layer, often referred to as the physical
    layer, pertains to the actual physical type and layout of wiring
    that provides the means for transmitting data.
    ```

    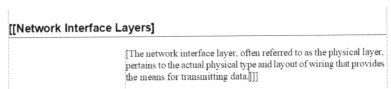

    [[Network Interface Layers]

    [The network interface layer, often referred to as the physical layer,
    pertains to the actual physical type and layout of wiring that provides
    the means for transmitting data.]]]

11. Press the **right arrow key**, once, to move out of the **Para** element.

12. Press the **Enter** key.

    The **Insert Element** dialog box displays at the insertion point in the **Structure View**, prompting you to type the name of the element you want to insert. Note that the **Figure, List, Note, Para, Section,** and **Table** elements display in the **Element Catalog** as a valid elements.

13. Start to type: `Section`

    Section is highlighted in the **Search** field as a valid element.

14. Press the **Enter** key.

    The **Section** element is inserted.

    A **Head** element is also automatically inserted.

    The **Structure View** indicates that you have inserted a Section element within a **Section** element.

    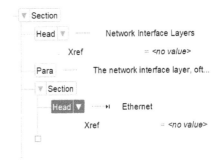

15. In the **Head** element, type: `Ethernet`

16. Press the **right arrow key**, once, to move out of the Head element.

17. Press the **Enter** key.

    The **Insert Element** dialog box displays at the insertion point in the **Structure View**, prompting you to type the name of the element you want to insert.

    Note that the **Para** element displays in the **Element Catalog** as a valid element.

18. Start to type: `Para`

    Para is highlighted in the **Search** field as a valid element.

19. Press the **Enter** key.

    The **Para** element is inserted.

20. In the **Para** element, type:

```
Ethernet can operate on three different cable types, and each
cable type has its limitations, requirements, specialized
components.
```

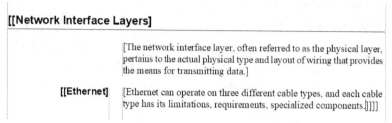

21. Select **File > Save** from the main menu, and then **File > Close**.

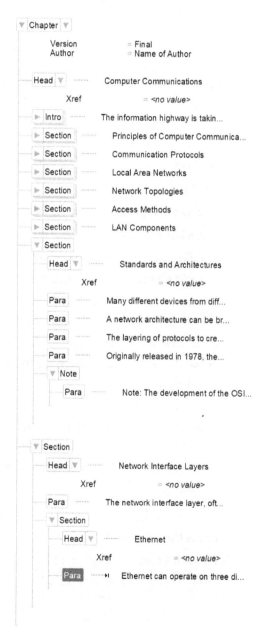

Chapter 9: Cross-references and Footnote Elements

Introduction

In this module, you will learn how to insert cross-reference elements. Then, after updating text, you will learn how to check for unresolved cross-references and updating cross-reference text.

You will also learn how to insert and edit the content in footnote elements.

Module Objectives

In this module, you will:

- Insert cross-reference elements.
- Fix unresolved cross-references.
- Insert footnote elements.

Cross-references

Cross-references refer the reader to related information in the current document, or another document.

When you insert a cross-reference element, you specify the:

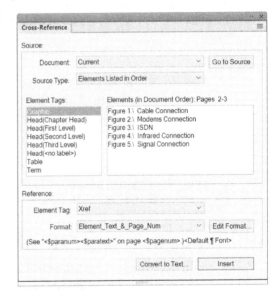

- Source document—either the current document or another open document.
- Source type—elements or paragraphs.
- Name of element or paragraph.
- Particular occurrence of the element or paragraph.
- Cross-reference format.

If you change the ID or move the source of a cross-reference, cross-references to that source will no longer be accurate. Periodically, you will update the cross-references in a document and correct any unresolved cross-references.

 The Cross-Reference panel displays options for both structured and unstructured cross-references. In structured documents you should refer to elements, rather than paragraphs.

Exercise 1:   Inserting sentence-based cross-reference elements

If defined in your template, cross-reference formats that insert a full sentence of information can make managing cross-references easier on you. In this exercise, you'll replace full sentences of content with a cross-reference containing everything you need in its place.

In this exercise, you will insert cross-reference elements that refer to graphic elements.

1. From the `AuthClass2020` directory, open `Chapter09.fm`.

2. If not already visible, open the **Structure View** and **Element Catalog**.

3. If not already visible, select **View > Borders**, then **View > Element Boundaries**.

4. On page 2 in the document window, click on the text in the first cell under the **Figure Reference** heading.

Table 1. **Connection Devices**

[Device]	[Connection media]	[Figure Reference]
[Computer]	[cable]	[[*(See "Figure 1. Cable Connection" on page 2.)*]]
[Modem]	[telephone line]	[(See "Figure 2. Modems Connection" on page 3.)]
[ISDN Terminator]	[telephone line]	[(See "Figure 3. ISDN" on page 3.)]
[Infrared]	[air]	[(See "Figure 4. Infrared Connection" on page 3.)]
[Signal]	[satellite]	[(See "Figure 5. Signal Connection" on page 3.)]

In this example, the cross-reference format used is responsible for italicizing the cross-reference text. Electronic cross-references allow for easier formatting of cross-references, versus manually entered text.

5. Note in the **Structure View** that rather than placing the cursor within a text string, you've selected an **Xref** element.

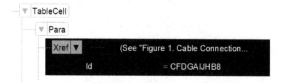

In this content model, a Para is required inside a table cell. If the cross-reference is the only content inside this cell, the cross-reference needs to be wrapped inside a Para element to create valid structure.

6. Place your cursor in the next cell down, in the *Figure 2* cross-reference.

You are able to insert the cursor directly into the text of this cross-reference information (and the other cells below it in this column) because the information was typed in manually, rather than inserted as electronic cross-references.

They will not update as an automatic part of your workflow so you'll replace them with **Xref** elements like the one in the previous row.

7. Double click on the snippet for the Figure 2 text-based cross-reference.

Double-clicking the snippet selects the content of the element without selecting the boundaries of the Para element itself.

8. Press the **Delete** key, or otherwise delete the existing text inside the Para element.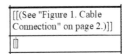

9. With your cursor inside the **Para** element, from the **Element Catalog**, select **Xref** and click the **Insert** button.

The **Cross-Reference** panel displays.

10. If not already selected, select **Current** from the **Document** drop-down menu.

11. If not already selected, select **Elements Listed in Order** from the **Source Type** drop-down menu.

    The **Element Tags** scroll list displays all element tags.

12. If not already selected, select **Graphic** from the **Element Tags** scroll list.

    The **Elements (in Document Order)** source text scroll list displays all occurrences of the selected element (**Graphic**) in the selected Document (**Current**).

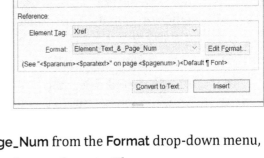

13. In the source text scroll list, select **Figure 2.\ Modems Connection.**

14. If not already selected, select **Element_Text_&_Page_Num** from the **Format** drop-down menu,

    The template designer has included several cross-reference formats. The "**Element_Text_&_Page_Num**" format will display the figure number, figure text, and figure page number in the text of the cross-reference.

15. Click the **Insert** button.

    The **Figure 2** cross-reference displays.

16. Following the previous steps, insert **Xref** elements to *Figure 3* through *Figure 5*, as shown.

17. Select **File > Save** from the main menu.

[Figure Reference]
[[(See "Figure 1. Cable Connection" on page 2.)]]
[[(See "Figure 2. Modems Connection" on page 3.)]]
[[(See "Figure 3. ISDN" on page 3.)]]
[[(See "Figure 4. Infrared Connection" on page 3.)]]
[[(See "Figure 5. Signal Connection" on page 3.)]]

Exercise 2:   Inserting phrase-based cross-reference elements

In this exercise, you will insert a cross-reference to a **Term** element.

1. On page 4 in the document, place the insertion point at the end of the **Para** element, above *Communication Protocols* as shown.

   to a digital signal that a computer can understand. This is the function of a modem.]]]

   [[Communication Protocols]

2. From the **Element Catalog**, select Xref and click the **Insert** button.

   The **Cross-Reference** panel displays.

3. From the **Element Tags** scroll list, select **Term**.

   The **Elements (in Document Order)** source text scroll list displays all occurrences of the **Term** element in the selected document.

4. In the source text scroll list, select **modem**.

5. If not selected, select the **See Term on pagenum (leading space)** format from the **Format** drop-down menu.

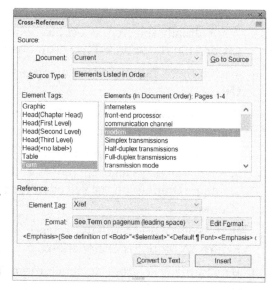

6. Click the **Insert** button.

   The cross-reference to *modem* displays in the text, and includes the leading space needed prior to the cross-reference.

   to a digital signal that a computer can understand. This is the function of a modem.[*(See definition of "modem" on page 4.)*]]]]

   [[Communication Protocols]

   In this case, the cross-reference is placed within an existing **Para** element, so you didn't need to place or wrap with a new **Para** element.

7. Select **File > Save** from the main menu.

Updating cross-references

Electronic cross-references update automatically, but not immediately. Information in cross-references will update in the following instances:

- Upon opening a document—FrameMaker checks the source of cross-references whenever you open a document. Availability of files and cross-referenced content will be confirmed, and the text of the cross-reference will be updated if needed.

- While updating a book—The Update Book dialog (covered in a later chapter) includes an option to update content in cross-references while updating other information across a book file.

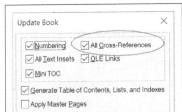

- When you invoke the **Edit > Update References** command— This dialog, used in the next exercise, allows you to update electronic cross-references and other contextual and referenced content.

Exercise 3:   Updating cross-references

In this exercise, you will modify your document by deleting the source content for a cross-reference. You will then update your cross-references and FrameMaker will alert you that there is an unresolved cross-reference. Afterward, you will learn to fix the unresolved cross-reference.

1. On page 2 in the document window, locate the third figure, *Figure 3. ISDN*, and place the insertion point in the figure's caption, *ISDN*.

   The **Structure View** refreshes to display the corresponding position within the **Structure View**.

   You may need to expand elements to view the **Figure**, **Caption**, and **Graphic** elements.

2. In the **Structure View**, select the parent **Figure** element.

   If you were to delete only the caption or graphic, the remaining structure would interfere with the other figures and captions.

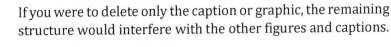

3. Press **Backspace** or **Delete**.

   The **Figure** element disappears. All remaining figures are renumbered. The *Infrared Connection* figure becomes *Figure 3*, and the *Signal Connection* figure becomes *Figure 4*.

4. On page **2** in the document window, locate the "**Connection Devices**" table.

   Note that the information from the *ISDN* cross-reference has not changed nor been removed.

   Cross-references do not automatically update when content changes are made.

   One way to update cross-reference information is to use the **Update References** command.

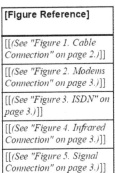

5. Select **Edit > Update References** from the main menu. The **Update References** dialog box displays.

6. Select (turn on) the **All Cross-References** check box.

7. Click **Update**.

The **Update Unresolved Cross-References** dialog box displays.

If the unresolved cross-reference had occurred because the source (the **Graphic** element) had been moved to a different document, this dialog allows you to specify a new location for the source.

Since the unresolved cross-reference was deleted and not misplaced, you will need correct it in a different way.

8. Click **Cancel** to close the dialog box.

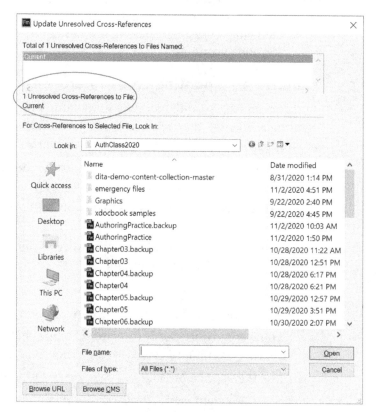

 Cross references update when opening documents, updating books, and when using the **Edit > Update References** command from the main menu.

 Exercise 4:   Locating an unresolved cross-reference

Unresolved electronic cross-references are searchable within FrameMaker. That makes them easy to locate using the **Find/Change** panel. In this exercise, you will use the **Find/Change** panel to locate the unresolved cross-reference.

1. Select **Edit > Find/Change** from the main menu.

The **Find/Change** dialog box displays.

2. From the **Find** menu, select
   Cross-Reference - Unresolved.

3. Click the **Find** button.

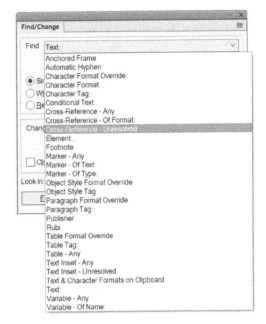

The unresolved cross-reference is highlighted.

In this case, the cross-reference is part of a
table row which is no longer relevant.

4. Select the **BodyRow** containing the unresolved
   cross-reference and delete it.

The unresolved cross-reference disappears.

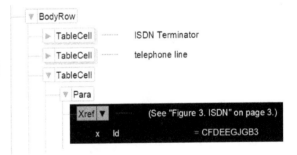

 If this reference to ISDN was to content that still existed, you might use the Cross-Reference panel to
recreate the reference to existing content rather than deleting the reference itself.

Exercise 5:   Navigating to the source of the cross-reference

In this exercise, you will use a shortcut to jump to a cross-reference's source.

1. On page 2 in the document window, locate the "**Connection Devices**" table.

2. Press **Ctrl + Alt** keys, then click on the cross-reference to *Figure 4* in the table.

The cross-reference link will highlight and FrameMaker jumps to the cross-reference source, *Figure 4* on page 3.

Table 1. Connection Devices		
[Device]	**[Connection media]**	**[Figure Reference]**
[Computer]	[cable]	[[*(See "Figure 1. Cable Connection" on page 2.)*]]
[Modem]	[telephone line]	[[*(See "Figure 2. Modems Connection" on page 3.)*]]
[ISDN Terminator]	[telephone line]	[[*(See "Figure 3. ISDN" on page 3.)*]]
[Infrared]	[air]	[[*(See "Figure 3. Infrared Connection" on page 3.)*]]
[Signal]	[satellite]	[[*(See "Figure 4. Signal Connection" on page 3.)*]]

Alternately, when a cross-reference is selected you can use the **Go To Source** button in the **Cross-Reference** panel to navigate to the source of a cross-reference.

As with other hyperlinks in FrameMaker, these links are passed as active links to PDF and online output (HTML and others) of your content.

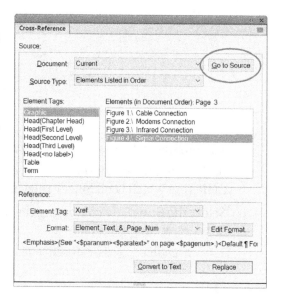

Footnotes

When you insert footnote elements, FrameMaker:

- Numbers the footnote, according to rules set by your template designer in your EDD.
- Formats the footnote text.
- Inserts a separator if the footnote is the first in a column, according to rules set by your template designer in your EDD.

As you edit the document, footnote numbering automatically updates.

Exercise 6:   Inserting footnote elements

In this exercise, you will add several **Footnote** elements and their text.

1. If not already open, open up the `Chapter09.fm` file from the `AuthClass2020` directory.

2. Navigate to the **Network Topologies** section and place the insertion point, as shown here.

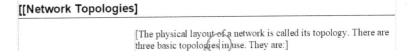

3. From the **Element Catalog**, select **Footnote** and click the **Insert** button.

   A **Footnote** element is inserted and the insertion point moves to the bottom of the page. Notice that FrameMaker numbers the first footnote with a "1".

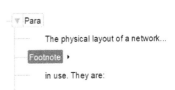

4. Type the following footnote text:

   ```
   You can also modify and combine characteristics of these "pure"
   network topologies to create hybrids.
   ```

   ---
   1.   You can also modify and combine characteristics of these "pure" network
   topologies to create hybrids.

5. Navigate to the LAN Components section using the structure view and place your cursor in the preceding paragraph, as shown.

   [A [**polling**] protocol requires an intelligent central device, such as a file server. If a workstation needs to transmit data, it sends the request to the file server when queried, or polled.]]

   Insertion point ─────

6. From the **Element Catalog**, select **Footnote** and click the **Insert** button.

   A **Footnote** element is inserted and the insertion point moves to the bottom of the page. Notice that FrameMaker numbers the footnote with a "2".

7. Type the following footnote text:

   ```
   This method is not as popular
   today as the other two methods.
   ```

   [The [**storage**] available on the file server is crucial. Both the size of the hard drive and the speed at which it provides access are important. Most network bottlenecks occur at the file server. Often,

   ---
   2.   This method is not as popular today as the other two methods.

8. Select **File > Save** from the main menu, and then **File > Close**.

Chapter 10: Anchored Frames and Imported Graphics

Introduction

In this module, you will become familiar with anchored frames in FrameMaker. You will also learn how to import and paste graphics.

Module Objectives

In this module, you will learn how to:

- Use the **Find/Change** window to locate an element.
- Use the **Find/Change** window to locate an anchored frame.
- Specify the anchoring position.
- Edit text preceding anchored frames.
- Insert and edit figure, graphic, and caption elements.
- Copy and paste a graphic into an anchored frame.
- Import a graphic by reference and by copy.

Graphic elements

A graphic element (the label may be something other than **Graphic**) is a container element that will insert a FrameMaker anchored frame into your text flow. Anchored frames reside in a specific location in the text flow, so when you edit the text preceding an anchored frame in the text flow, the frame and everything in it moves accordingly. With anchored frames, you don't have to reposition graphics each time you edit text.

In this specific structure model, you will place anchored frames for your graphics by inserting a **Graphic** element inside of a **Figure** element.

 Exercise 1:   Finding an element

When using the **Find/Change** feature in structured documents, you have the option to search for specific elements and the option to search for elements with specific attribute values. This can dramatically improve the efficiency of your **Find/Change** usage.

In this exercise, you will use the **Find/Change** command to locate a **Figure** element. However, if you needed to, you could also narrow your search results to find only **Figure** elements with specific **Type** attribute values.

1. From the `AuthClass2020` directory, open `Chapter10.fm`.
2. If not already visible, open the **Structure View** and **Element Catalog**.
3. If not already visible, show **Borders**, and **Element Boundaries**.

4. Select **Edit > Find/Change** from the main menu.
   The **Find/Change** dialog displays.

5. From the **Find** menu, select **Element**.

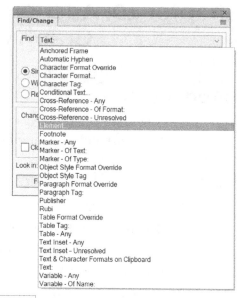

The **Find Element** dialog displays.

6. Type `Figure` in the **Element Tag** field.

7. Click the **Set** button.

 If **Element** is already visible in the **Find** field, you'll need to reselect it to see the **Find Element** dialog.

8. In the **Find/Change** dialog, click the **Find** button.
   The first **Figure** element, *Figure 1* is selected.

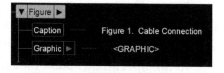

When searching for elements, text entered into the field below **Element** will not be used in the search.

9. Continue clicking the **Find** button until **Figure 4. Signal Connection** is highlighted.

In the **Structure View**, the **Figure** element is selected.

Notice that the **Figure** element has two child elements: **Caption** and **Graphic**. The **Graphic** element contains the anchored frame.

Exercise 2: Finding an anchored frame

In addition to searching for structure, you can also choose to search for FrameMaker objects.

In this exercise, you will use the **Find/Change** command to find the next anchored frame.

Because the anchored frame is represented by a **Graphic** element, this is similar to what you might achieve by searching for an element named **Graphic**.

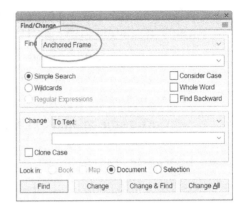

1. In the **Find/Change** dialog box, select **Anchored Frame** from the **Find** drop-down menu.

2. Click the **Find** button.

   FrameMaker finds the next anchored frame and highlights the anchored frame symbol (if Text Symbols are showing) and frame.

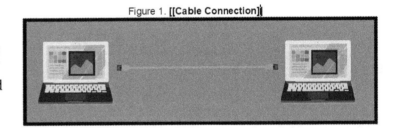
Figure 1. [[Cable Connection]]

   If needed, expand the **Structure View** until you can see that **Graphic** is the selected element.

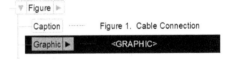

3. Close the **Find/Change** window.

Exercise 3: Editing paragraphs containing anchored frames

In this exercise, you will edit the text preceding an anchored frame and observe how the anchored frame repositions automatically.

1. On page 2 in the document window, place the insertion point at the end of the **Para** element preceding the table.

2. Press the **Enter** key one or more times to create blank **Para** elements. As you do, **Table 1** and the figures that follow drop down to accommodate your new content.

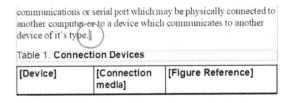

 If you see the Smart Insert for Elements dialog display, you are outside of the Para element, not at the end of the para element.

3. Return to the previous state by deleting the new Para elements you just entered.

   You can delete the new elements by using **Undo**, the **Backspace** key, or deleting them from the **Structure View**.

   Notice that *Figure 1* returns to page 2.

Creating an anchored frame

When you insert an anchored frame/graphic element, you specify the anchoring position for the frame in relation to the insertion point:

- Below current line—directly below the insertion point.
- At the top or bottom of the column containing the insertion point
- At the insertion point—in the line of text
- Outside the column containing the insertion point—anchored frame may still be within the overall text frame
- Outside the text frame containing the insertion point—in the margin of the page.
- Run into paragraph

The following graphic depicts several anchoring positions.

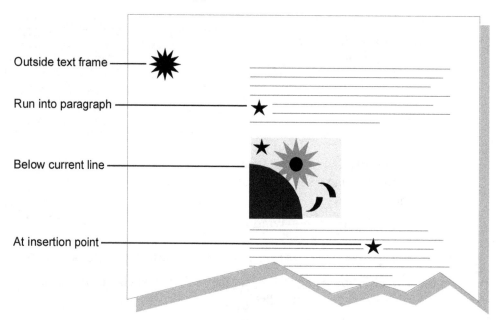

Adding Graphics

You can place one *or more* types of graphics inside each anchored frame by:

- Drawing with the drawing tools.
- Copying or cutting and pasting the graphic from the current (or another) document.
- Importing from another file.

In the structured document used in these exercises, the **Figure** element has a **Type** attribute which controls whether the **Anchored Frame** dialog or the **Import File** dialog appears when you insert the **Graphic** element.

The **Anchored Frame** dialog box lets you specify the anchoring position and size of a placeholder frame. After inserting an anchored frame as a placeholder, you can drag, draw, paste, or import one or more graphics into the frame.

The **Import File** dialog box lets you specify a file to import, without first specifying the anchoring position and size of the frame. When you import the graphic, FrameMaker automatically creates a frame below the current line, centered in the text column, and sizes the frame to fit the imported graphic.

Importing by copy

To import a copy of the graphic, click the **Copy File into Document** radio button. FrameMaker stores the file internally in your FrameMaker file. If you store files in .xml or .dita format, this may not be an option. By copying into document, FrameMaker does not maintain a link between the graphic in the document and the original graphic file.

There is one advantage of copying a file into a document: It's easier to move or copy documents to another location. Because all graphics are in the document—not in separate files—you don't have to move or copy them along with the document.

There are also several disadvantages to this approach:

- The document's size will increase dramatically.
- You will use more disk space because copies of the graphic are stored both in the file on disk.
- Later, if you change the source used for the graphic file, the graphic in the document isn't updated. You must import the graphic again to update it.

Setting bitmap resolution

If the graphic you import is a bitmap, the scale you choose in the **Object Properties** dialog, along with the the pixels per inch (PPI) of the image determine the space the image occupies on the page. The value you specify determines the amount of space the graphic occupies on the page, and the higher the pixels displayed per inch, the cleaner the graphic will display.

Original AI file   SVG   288 dpi PNG   144 dpi PNG   72 dpi PNG

 The AI and SVG files above are vector images, so in PDF the images will be smooth at any scale, and in print, the resolution will be optimized for the output device used.

There are multiple ways to place graphics; after importing you can control the scale or resolution of a bitmap (changing either will impact the other) via the **Object Properties** panel.

Exercise 4:   Creating placeholders for graphic elements

In this exercise, you will insert an anchored frame element and copy and paste a graphic into the frame.

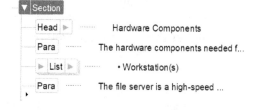

1. Using the **Structure View**, place your cursor at the end of the **Hardware Components** section. **Hardware Components** should be on page 7 of `Chapter10.fm`.

    The **Document View** scrolls to remain in sync with the new insertion point.

2. From the **Element Catalog**, select **Figure** and click the **Insert** button.

   The **Attributes for New Element** dialog box displays.

3. In the **Attribute Name** scroll list, select **Type**.

4. From the **Value** drop-down menu, select **Pasted**.

5. Click the **Insert Element** button.

The **Figure** element displays in the **Structure View**.

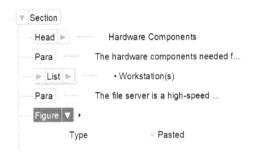

6. From the **Element Catalog**, select **Caption** and click the **Insert** button.

   The **Caption** element displays.

7. Type My Pasted Graphic into the **Caption** element.

   Figure 5. displays, followed by the title *My Pasted Graphic*.

8. In the **Structure View**, click directly below the **Caption** element.

9. From the **Element Catalog**, select **Graphic** and click the **Insert** button.

   Because you earlier chose to mark the figure as **Pasted**, or *to be pasted later*, FrameMaker opens the (or highlights the already open) **Anchored Frame** panel, giving you the ability to insert a placeholder frame into your document.

10. In the **Anchored Frame** panel, ensure:

    a. Anchoring position is set to **Below Current Line**

    b. Alignment is set to **Center**

    c. Width is set to **6.125"**

    d. Height is set to **1.8"**

11. Click the **New Frame** button.

Depending on your **New Element Options** settings, the **Attributes for New Element** dialog box may display, requesting a value for the ID attribute.

If you already knew the name of the graphic to insert, you could enter it here and avoid adding the missing value later in the validation process.

For now you'll leave it blank.

12. Click the **Insert Element** button.

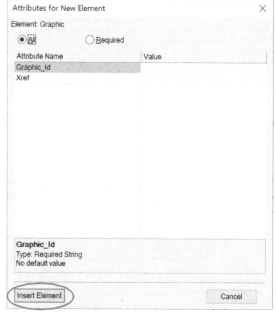

The **Graphic** element displays in the **Structure View**, and a corresponding empty frame displays in the **Document View**.

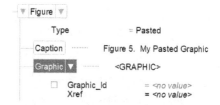

13. From the `AuthClass2020` directory, open `Chapter10 file with graphic.fm`.

14. Click on the graphic contained in `Chapter10 file with graphic.fm` to select it.

    When selected, handles appear on the border around the graphic.

15. Copy the graphic to the clipboard.

16. In `Chapter10.fm`, click on the border of the anchored frame in *Figure 5* to select it.

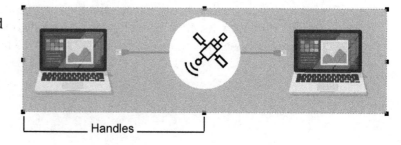

17. Select **Edit > Paste** from the main menu.

    The graphic is pasted into the frame and centered both horizontally and vertically.

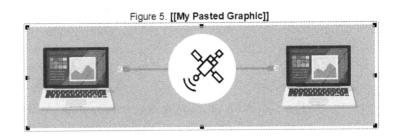

Figure 5. **[[My Pasted Graphic]]**

 If this image was a file on disk, rather than an image stored in another document you could do the following: After selecting the dotted line of your graphic frame, use the **File>Import>File** dialog to directly import the image from its location. You'll see a variation on this in the next exercise.

Importing by reference

To import a graphic by reference, click the **Import by Reference** option in the **Import File** dialog box. FrameMaker inserts a screen view of the graphic and stores a reference to the graphic, not the graphic itself. If the original graphic imported by reference is changed, FrameMaker updates the document the next time the FrameMaker file is opened or updated.

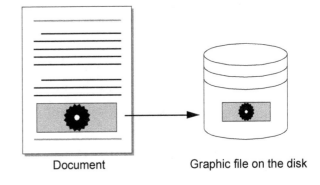

Document   Graphic file on the disk

There are advantages to importing by reference:

- You can quickly change the graphic in a document by editing the original graphic file.
- You can use the same graphic file in several documents and update from one central location.

  For example, if you have a graphic file containing your company logo, you can use it in letters, memos, reports, and presentations. You can update all documents containing the logo by changing a single graphic file.

- You conserve disk space because there is only one copy of the graphic on the disk.

Disadvantages of importing by reference:

- You are responsible for organizing and maintaining the graphic files in appropriate locations.

  For example, if you move a document containing referenced graphics you'll need to relink the graphics within FrameMaker.

  FrameMaker's **File>Package** command can help you collect the files into a ZIP file prior to changing project location for easier management.

Exercise 5:   Importing by reference

In this exercise, you will insert a **Figure** element with the **Type** attribute set to **Imported**, resulting in display of the **Import** dialog box. You will choose to **Import (file) by Reference**, rather than **Import by Copy**.

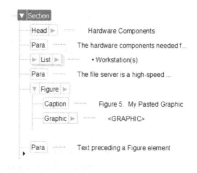

1. In the **Structure View**, place the insertion point below (not inside) the **Figure** element you just finished with.

2. Insert a **Para** element, and type `Text preceding a Figure element.`

3. In the **Structure View**, place your cursor below the newly entered paragraph.

4. From the **Element Catalog**, select **Figure** and click the **Insert** button.

   The **Attributes for New Element** dialog box displays.

5. Set the value of the **Type** attribute to **Imported**.

6. Click the **Insert Element** button.

   The **Figure** element displays.

7. In the **Element Catalog**, select **Caption** and click the **Insert** button.

   The **Caption** element displays in the **Structure View** and **Figure 6** displays in the document window.

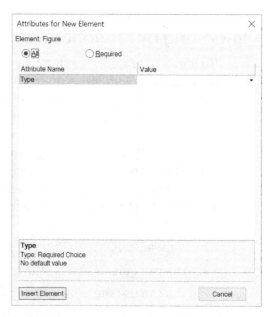

8. In the **Caption** element, type:
   `My Figure Imported by Reference`

   Figure 6 is displayed in the **Structure View**, followed by the rest of the snippet.

9. In the **Structure View**, click directly below the **Caption** element.

10. From the **Element Catalog**, select **Graphic** and click the **Insert** button.

The **Import** dialog box displays.

11. In the **Import** dialog box, navigate to the `AuthClass2020\Graphics` directory.

12. Select the `cable.pdf` file.

13. Select (click) the **Import by Reference** radio button.

14. Click the **Import** button.

Because the imported graphic is a vector file, the size is determined by the parameters of the file.

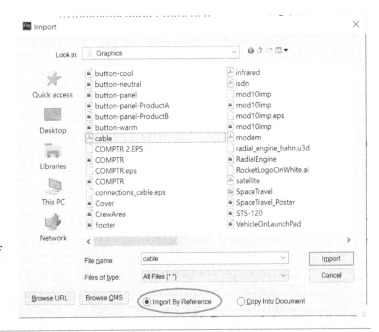

 Starting with FrameMaker 2017, if you import an image wider than the available column, FrameMaker will automatically reduce the scale of the image to fit within the column. If this happens you can manually resize the image by selecting the graphic and adjusting the sizing handles or by using the Object Properties panel. For a video showing this behavior, see https://vimeo.com/mattrsullivan/review/197462249/8424c5c60a

The **Graphic** element displays in the **Structure View**.

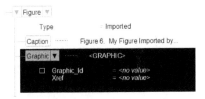

In the document window, the graphic is inserted into an anchored frame underneath the **Figure 6** title. You can now control the size of the graphic with the **Object Properties** panel.

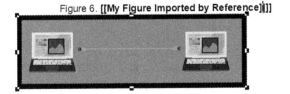

Figure 6. [[My Figure Imported by Reference]]]]

15. To adjust the size of the anchored frame, select the anchored frame border (the dotted line around the figure) and in the **Anchored Frame** panel, set the **Width** to `6.125″` and the **Height** to `1.8″` and click **Edit Frame**.

The anchored frame now more closely fits the width of the column.

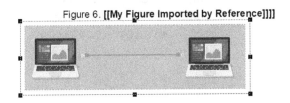

Figure 6. [[My Figure Imported by Reference]]]]

If your measurement preferences are set to something other than Inches, the units you typed in will be converted and displayed according to your document preferences.

16. If you'd like to change the size of your placed graphic, select the image itself and then shift-drag a corner or use the **Object Properties** panel to set the **Width** and **Height** (or **Scaling**) values as needed. In this example, a **Width** of 6″ (with **Preserve Aspect Ratio** selected) will give you and image that is approximately the same width of the other images in this lesson.

17. Select **File > Save** from the main menu.

18. Practice your importing skills by bringing the file in using **Copy into Document**, rather than **Import by Reference** to see how close the two options are in practice.

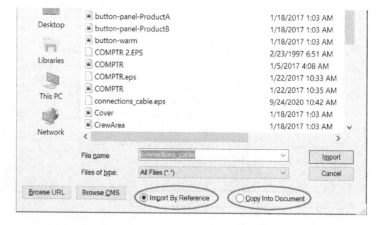

Chapter 11: Tables

Introduction

In this module, you will learn how to insert table elements and modify tables. You will also learn how to customize the appearance of an individual cell and insert a table footnote element.

Module Objectives

In this module you will learn how to:

- Insert table elements.
- Set the initial number of rows and columns of the new table.
- Move around in tables.
- Add elements and text to table cells.
- Select table parts.
- Change column widths.
- Add and delete rows and columns.
- Add table footnotes.
- Straddle table cells.
- Apply custom ruling and shading to cells.

Using Tables

A table organizes information into *cells* arranged in *rows* and *columns*. Structured table elements occupy a specific position within structure. As a result, when text moves, the table also moves.

Table formats can specify properties, such as the table's alignment in the text frame (left, center, right), space above and below the entire table, rulings separating rows and/or columns, shading of rows or columns, and so on. Many of the formatting options for these table parts are beyond the scope of this workbook and would be created by the template designer.

See my FrameMaker reference book, *FrameMaker - Working with Content* for information on setting up table formats, or *www.techcommtools.com* for available template design courses.

Basic table structure

The table element defined in this chapter can include the following children:

- **TableTitle** (optional)
- **TableHeading** (optional)
- **TableBody** (required)
- **TableFooting** (optional)

Generally, table child elements may also have children:

- **TableTitle**—Contains text, has no children
- **TableHeading**—1 or more row elements
- **TableBody**—1 or more row elements
- **TableFooting**—1 or more row elements

Device	Connection media	Figure Reference
Computer	cable	*(See "Figure 1. Cable Connection" on page 2.)*
Modem	telephone line	*(See "Figure 2. Modems Connection" on page 3.)*
ISDN Terminator	telephone line	*(See "Figure 3. ISDN" on page 3.)*
Infrared	air	*(See "Figure 3. Infrared Connection" on page 3.)*
Signal	satellite	*(See "Figure 4. Signal Connection" on page 3.)*

Table 1. **Connection Devices**

TableTitle — Table 1. **Connection Devices**

Table Heading — Device / Connection media / Figure Reference

Table Body

Table Footing — Each connection media has its own advantages. Consider your network requirements before implementation.

Each of the row elements must have one or more cell elements. Each of the cell elements can contain directly-typed text, child elements, or a combination of text and children.

Text is typed only in the **TableTitle** element and cell elements, or children of cell elements.

If the table extends to more than one page, these elements, if present, will repeat on every page:

- **TableTitle**
- **TableHeading**
- **TableFooting**

A table's structure might look like this:

 Exercise 1: Inserting a table element

In this exercise, you will insert a table element.

1. From the `AuthClass2020` directory, open `Chapter11.fm`.
2. If not already open, open the **Structure View** and the **Element Catalog**.
3. If not already selected, select **View > Borders** and **View > Text Symbols** from the main menu.
4. Navigate to the bottom of the **Structure View** and click directly below the **Para** element at the end of the document.

   The **Document View** scrolls to remain in sync with the document window.

5. In the **Element Catalog,** select **Table** and click the **Insert** button.

   The **Attributes for New Element** dialog box displays.

6. In the **Attribute Name** column, select **Type.**

7. In the **Value** column, click the down arrow and select **Features Table.**

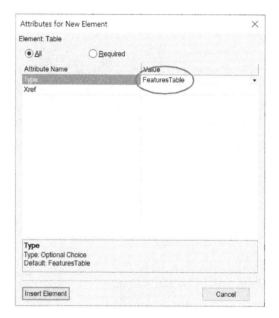

8. Click the **Insert Element** button.

   The **Insert Table** dialog box displays.

9. Enter the number of columns and rows:

   - Columns: 3
   - Body Rows: 5
   - Heading Rows: 1
   - Footing Rows: 0

10. Click the **Table Format** down arrow and select **Features Table** from the list.

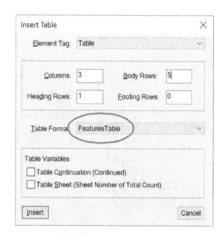

11. Click the **Insert** button.

A blank table appears in the document window.

The template designer for this document previously created table formats with initial column, body row, heading row, and footing row settings. You can override these values in the Insert Table dialog box Column, Body Rows, Heading Rows, or Footing Rows fields. You can also add or delete table parts after the table is inserted.

In the **Structure View**, the table's initial structure displays. Notice the new table has two parts; a **TableHeading** and **TableBody**. The missing table title will be added later.

12. Select **File > Save** from the main menu.

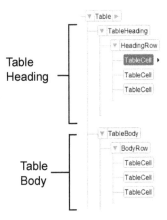

Moving Around in a Table

You can move around in a table using the mouse, or a keyboard equivalent (**Tab**, **Shift + Tab**, or arrow keys).

Next cell§	Tab§
Previous cell§	Shift + Tab§
Cell below§	Down arrow§
Cell above§	Up arrow§

⚠ Navigation shortcuts may be different in versions of FrameMaker before the 2017 release.

Exercise 2:   Moving from cell to cell

In this exercise, you will practice moving the insertion point from cell to cell, using the keyboard.

1. Click in the first cell.

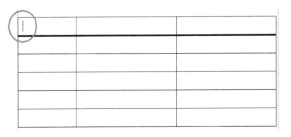

2. Press **Tab** once, to move to the next cell in the row.

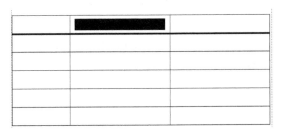

In a cell, pressing **Tab** moves to the next cell. To insert a tab in the cell, use the combination **Esc + Tab**.

3. Press **Shift + Tab** once, to return to the first cell in the row.

4. Practice using the keyboard equivalents, shown above, to move around in the table.

    If moving a long distance, it may be easier to just click inside the cell.

Selecting Parts of a Table

Selecting within a cell

To select the following within a cell:

- A word—Double-click the word.
- A range of text—Click and drag the mouse cursor I-beam over the range of words.
- An element
    - Drag the mouse cursor I-beam over the element boundary, or
    - Select an element bubble in the **Structure** View.

The following figure displays the selection of text within an element in a cell.

[Device]	[Connection media]	[Figure Reference]
[Computer]	[cable]	[[See "Cable Connection" on page 2.]]

The following figure displays the selection of an element in a cell.

[Device]	[Connection media]	[Figure Reference]
[Computer]	[cable]	[[See "Cable Connection" on page 2.]]

As you select elements and text in cells, the current element name is displayed in the status bar.

Flow: A E: ... > Section > Section > Table > TableBody > BodyRow > TableCell

Selecting cells

Do one of the following to select an entire cell:

- Click in the cell and drag the mouse cursor from border to border of the cell.
- Select the **Cell** element in the **Structure** View.
- **Ctrl+click** inside the cell.

The following figure displays the selection of a cell:

To extend the selection of cells:

Press **Ctrl + Shift** + click in the cell(s).

[Device]	[Connection media]	[Figure Reference]
[Computer]	[cable]	[[See "Cable Connection" on page 2.]]

As you select cells, the status bar updates to describe your position and selection.

Flow: A E: Chapter > Section > Section > Table > TableBody > BodyRow

If you drag from heading, footing, or body of a table to another table part, entire rows and/or columns are selected.

 ## Exercise 3:   Selecting rows and columns

Do one of the following to select a row:

- Click in the first cell of the row and drag the cursor across all of cells in the row.
- Select the **BodyRow** element in the **Structure View**.
- **Ctrl+double-click** on a vertical line within a row.

Do one of the following to select a column:

- Click in the first cell in the column and drag the mouse cursor down the column.
- Press **Ctrl** + double-click on a column's horizontal border.

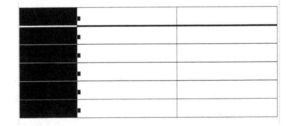

Do one of the following to select the entire table:

- Select the entire cell, right-click, and select **Select All of Table** from the menu.
- Select the **Table** element in the **Structure View**.
- **Ctrl +triple-click** anywhere in the table.

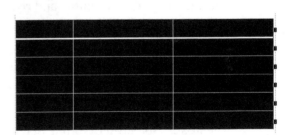

Column Width and Row Height

You can manually resize a column width—make it narrower or wider—by selecting it and dragging its cell's right-edge resize handle to the left or right, respectively. The table width will change by the amount you drag.

Table 2. Advantages and Disadvantages of topologies

[]	[Advantages]	[Disadvantages]
[Star]	[Easy to service] [Cable layout is easy to modify]	[Large amount of cabling is required to connect the network] [A single hub means that if the hub fails, then the entire network fails.]

—Drag resize handle to change width

Column width can also be changed by selecting **Table > Resize Columns** from the main menu.

 Exercise 4:   Changing column width

In this exercise, you will adjust the column widths of the first and second column.

1. Select the first cell in the second column.

    A resize handle displays on the right side of the cell.

2. If needed, display rulers using **View > Rulers**.

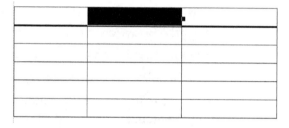

3. Reduce the column width by dragging the handle to the left and continue holding the mouse button down.

    You see the cell's left, center, and right margins change in the ruler area, as you drag the cell's handle.

Cell's left, center and right margins are circled below

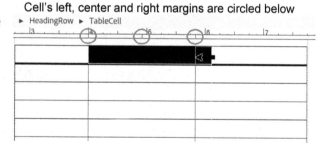

4. Select the first cell in the last column.

5. Select **Table > Resize Columns** from the main menu.

    The **Resize Selected Columns** dialog box displays.

6. If not on already selected, click (turn on) the **To Width** radio button.

7. Click in the **To Width** text box, and type: `1"`

    If you don't include the inch symbol, the dialog will use the default units for this document.

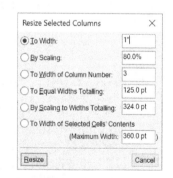

8. Click the **Resize** button.

    The column is now 1 inch wide.

9. Select **File > Save** from the main menu.

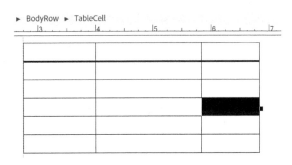

Modifying Table Structure

A table's structure is modified by adding or deleting table rows and columns. To add rows:

*   Copy and paste other rows.
*   With insertion point in the cell, press **Ctrl** (key) + **Enter** (key); one row is added below the row containing the insertion point.
*   Use **Table > Add Rows or Columns** command from the main menu.
*   Insert **Row** elements in the **Structure View**.

To add columns, copy and paste other columns, or use the **Table > Add Rows or Columns** command from the main menu.

When a table's rows extend beyond a page, the table title, heading row(s), and footing row(s) are automatically recreated on every new page of the table. To force a break on a specific body row, position your cursor in the row and use the **Table > Format >Row Format** command.

Deleting rows, columns, and cells

Rows and columns are deleted from a table using basic editing commands. After selecting an entire row or column, press **Delete** or select **Edit > Clear** from the main menu. If an entire row or column is not selected, the contents of the selected cells will be deleted and the row or column will remain in the table.

 Exercise 5: Deleting a column

In this exercise, you will delete the last column.

1. Select the third column in the table.

2. Press the **Delete** key.

    The **Clear Table Cells** dialog box displays.

3. Select (turn on) the **Remove Cells from Table** radio button.

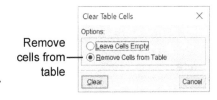

Remove cells from table

 If the Clear Table Cells dialog box does not display, check to ensure that an entire column is selected.

4. Click the **Clear** button.

    The column is deleted.

5. Select the first column.

6. Select **Table > Resize Columns** from the main menu.

The **Resize Selected Columns** dialog box displays.

7. If not on already, select (turn on) the **To Width** radio button.

8. In the **To Width** text box, type: `1.25"`

9. Click the **Resize** button.

   The first column resizes to 1.25 inches.

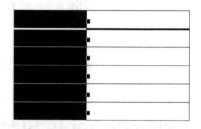

10. Using the same method, resize the second column to 3.25".

11. Select **File > Save** from the main menu.

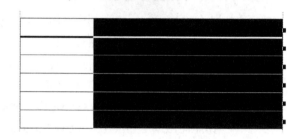

 Exercise 6:   Deleting rows

Similar to the previous exercise, you will delete a few rows from your table.

1. Select the bottom three rows of your table.

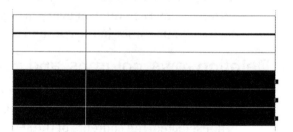

2. Press the **Delete** key.

   The **Clear Table Cells** dialog box displays.

3. Select (turn on) the **Remove Cells from Table** radio button.

Remove cells from table

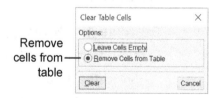

 If the Clear Table Cells dialog box does not display, check to ensure that full rows are selected.

4. Click the **Clear** button.

   The row is deleted.

In the next exercise, you'll learn various ways to add rows back into the table.

Exercise 7:   Adding rows

In this exercise, you will add a row to your table, by selecting **Table > Add Rows or Columns** from the main menu.

1. Place the insertion point in the last row in the table, in either cell.

2. Select **Table > Add Rows or Columns** from the main menu.

   The **Add Rows or Columns** dialog box displays.
   Set the following options:

   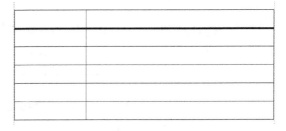

   - If not already on, select (turn on) the **Add Rows** radio button.

   - In the **Add Rows** text box, type: 3

   - Click the **Add Rows** drop-down arrow and select **Below Selection**.

3. Click the **Add** button.

   Below the row containing the insertion point, three rows are added to the table.

4. Delete the three rows you just added.

5. In the **Structure View**, position your cursor at the end of the **TableBody** element.

6. From the **Element Catalog**, insert a **BodyRow** element.

   A BodyRow element appears, along with two TableCell elements.

7. Place your cursor in either cell of the last row.

8. Press **Control+Return** to add another row.

   A blank row appears.

9. Place your cursor in the last cell of the table.

10. Press **Tab** on your keyboard to add another row to the table.

    A blank row appears.

 Adding body rows using the shortcuts shown above gives the same structure as adding rows from the element catalog, so use whichever method you find most comfortable.

11. Select **File > Save** from the main menu.

Exercise 8:   Adding a table title

In this exercise, you will add a **TableTitle** element and enter the table's title.

1. In the **Structure View**, place the insertion point above the **TableHeading** element.

2. In the **Element Catalog**, select **TableTitle** and click the **Insert** button.

    The **TableTitle** element displays in the **Structure View**.

    A table title area is added to the table.

    Notice that the table title is autonumbered and that the insertion point is placed after the table title number.

3. In the **TableTitle** element, type: `OSI Model`

    The table title numbers automatically, and the value depends upon how many previous **TableTitle** elements are found in this chapter.

4. Delete the last two rows of the table and select **File > Save** from the main menu.

Adding elements and text to table cells

To add text to a table, you insert elements and type text in the elements. As you type text in a cell, the cell's height resizes automatically to hold the text.

 Exercise 9:   Adding elements and text in table cells

In this exercise, you will add elements and text to the table.

Your finished table will look like the example shown here:

1. If not already visible, display **Element Boundaries** from the **View** menu.

2. Place the insertion point in the first cell in the table. Note that this is in a **HeadingRow** element.

3. In the **Element Catalog**, select **Head** and click the **Insert** button.

    The **Attributes for New Element** dialog typically displays.

    Head elements have an attribute called **Xref** used in cross-referencing, but this is an optional attribute and you can ignore it for now.

4. Click the **Insert Element** button.

    The **Head** element is inserted.

5. In the **Head** element, type: `Term`

6. Repeat the steps for the **Description** heading as shown.

Table 4. **OSI Model**

[Term]	[Description]
[Layer 1 Physical Layer]	[Responsible for transmitting bit streams across a particular physical transmission medium.]
[Layer 2 Data Link Layer]	[Provides reliable data transmission from one node to another, and shields the higher layers from any concerns regarding the physical transmission of data.]
[Layer 3 Network Layer]	[Routes data from one network node to another.] [Responsible for establishing, maintaining, and terminating the network connection between two users.]

Table 4. **OSI Model**

[Term]	[Description]

Exercise 10: Prompting for required attribute values only

To speed up entry of content, in this exercise, you will suppress prompting for optional attributes.

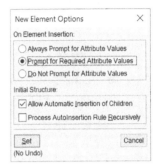

1. Select **Element > New Element Options** from the main menu.
   The **New Element Options** dialog box displays.

2. Choose the **Prompt for Required Attribute Values** radio button.

3. Click the **Set** button.

4. Select **File > Save** from the main menu.

 Exercise 11: Practicing inserting table elements and text

In this exercise, you will continue to add elements and text to the table.

1. Click in the first cell in the second row.

2. In the **Element Catalog**, select **Head** and click the **Insert** button.
   Note that the **Attributes for ' Element** dialog box does not display.

3. In the **Head** element, type: Layer 1 Physical Layer

4. Press **Tab** to move to the next cell.

5. In the **Element Catalog**, select **Para** and click the **Insert** button.

6. In the **Para** element, type:

   ```
   Responsible for transmitting bit
   streams across a particular
   physical transmission medium.
   ```

   The first body row of your table is complete.

7. Select **File > Save** from the main menu.

8. Continue inserting Head elements in the left column and Para elements in the right column to complete the table, as shown.

9. Select **File > Save** from the main menu.

Table 4. **OSI Model**

[Term]	[Description]
[Layer 1 Physical Layer]	[Responsible for transmitting bit streams across a particular physical transmission medium.]
[Layer 2 Data Link Layer]	[Provides reliable data transmission from one node to another, and shields the higher layers from any concerns regarding the physical transmission of data.]
[Layer 3 Network Layer]	[Routes data from one network node to another.] [Responsible for establishing, maintaining, and terminating the network connection between two users.]

Inserting table footnotes

Table footnotes are structured elements which appear immediately below the table. When a table footnote element is inserted in a table cell, the insertion point moves to the footnote area below the table and is ready for input.

 Exercise 12: Adding a table footnote element

In this exercise, you will insert a table footnote element and its text.

1. In the last cell of the table, place the insertion point after the period following the word *users*.

2. In the **Element Catalog**, select **Footnote** and click the **Insert** button.

   The **Footnote** element is inserted, and the insertion point moves to the footnote area, at the bottom of the table.

3. In the **Footnote** element, type:

   ```
   Network monitoring software
   packages continuously monitor
   this layer.
   ```

4. Select **File > Save** from the main menu.

[Layer 3 Network Layer]	[Routes data from one network node to another.] [Responsible for establishing, maintaining, and terminating the network connection between two users.]

[Layer 3 Network Layer]	[Routes data from one network node to another.] [Responsible for establishing, maintaining, and terminating the network connection between two users.[a]]

a. Network monitoring software packages continuously monitor this layer.

Stradding cells, rows and columns

You can select cells, rows, columns, or a block of cells, and merge them into a single cell that extends across the width of the original cells. Any number of adjacent cells of the same type (heading, body, or footing) can be combined with a straddle.

 Exercise 13: Straddling table cells

In this exercise, you will insert a footing row and then straddle the **TableCell** elements to allow a **Para** element to flow across the entire width of the row.

1. Place the insertion point below the **TableBody** in the **Structure View**.

2. Add a **TableFooting** element.

   A **TableFooting** element and two **TableCell** elements are inserted.

3. Drag across the new row to select both cells.

4. Select **Table > Straddle** from the main menu.

   The selected cells in the last row are straddled and become one cell.

5. Place the insertion point in the straddled row.

6. In the **Element Catalog**, select **Para** and click the **Insert** button.

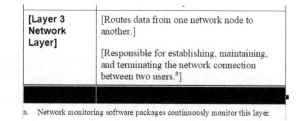

a. Network monitoring software packages continuously monitor this layer.

7. In the **Para** element, type:

   ```
   The OSI Model's three layers
   form the foundation of network
   communication.
   ```

8. Select **File > Save** from the main menu.

[Layer 3 Network Layer]	[Routes data from one network node to another.]
	[Responsible for establishing, maintaining, and terminating the network connection between two users.[a]]
The OSI Model's three layers form the foundation of network communication.	

a. Network monitoring software packages continuously monitor this layer.

 You can also select the TableFooting row or select both TableCell elements in the Structure View to straddle cells.

Custom Cell Formatting

Custom Ruling and Shading lets you apply shading and ruling on individual cells or groups of cells. This custom ruling and changing lets you format individual cells by overriding the ruling and shading applied by the table's overall format, meaning that the changes will not be stored in .xml or .dita files.

 While format overrides are possible when working with structured content in FrameMaker, overrides are generally not a good idea and should be avoided.

 ### Exercise 14: (Optional) Applying custom shading to cells

In this exercise, you will apply custom shading to cells in a table.

1. Locate the "**Advantages and Disadvantages of Cabling**" table near the end of the `mod11.fm` document.

2. Select the first cell under the **Advantages** heading in the second column as shown.

3. Select **Table > Custom Ruling and Shading** from the main menu.

Table 3. **Advantages and Disadvantages of Cabling**

[]	[Advantages]	[Disadvantages]
[Co-axial cable]	• [[[Can run unboosted for longer distances than twisted-pair cable]] • [[Can transmit voice, video, and data]] • [[Technology used is standard]]]	• [[[Rigid cables may cause difficulty installing]] • [[More expensive than twisted-pair cable]]]
[Twisted-pair cable]	• [[[Low in cost]] • [[Easy to connect devices]]]	• [[[More prone to interference than coaxial or fiber-optic cable]]

The **Custom Ruling and Shading** window displays.

4. Deselect (turn off) the **Custom Cell Ruling** check box and select (turn on) the **Custom Cell Shading** check box.

5. Click the **Fill** drop-down arrow and select **10%** from the menu.

6. Click the **Color** drop-down arrow and select **Red**.

7. Click the **Apply** button.

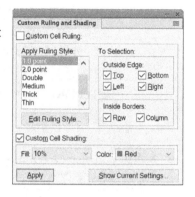

8. Click anywhere outside the cell to deselect it. Notice the red shading on the cell.

9. Select **File > Save** from the main menu.

[]	[Advantages]	[Disadvantages]
[Co-axial cable]	• [[[Can run unboosted for longer distances than twisted-pair cable]] • [[Can transmit voice, video, and data]] • [[Technology used is standard]]]	• [[[Rigid cables may cause difficulty installing]] • [[More expensive than twisted-pair cable]]]
[Twisted-pair cable]	• [[[Low in cost]] • [[Easy to connect	• [[[More prone to interference than

Table 3. **Advantages and Disadvantages of Cabling**

 Exercise 15: Applying custom ruling to cells

In this exercise, you will apply custom ruling to the *Twisted-Pair cable* row.

1. In either the **Document** View or the **Structure View**, select the *Twisted-Pair cable* row.

2. In the **Custom Ruling and Shading** dialog box, select (turn on) the **Custom Cell Ruling** check box and deselect (turn off) the **Custom Cell Shading** check box.

   Since the **Custom Cell Shading** options are not selected, the **Fill** and **Color** settings will not be applied.

3. In the **Apply Ruling Style** scroll list, select **2.0 point**.

4. In the **To Selection** area, select (turn on) the **Top**, **Left**, **Bottom**, and **Right** check boxes.

5. If not already deselected, deselect (turn off) the **Row** and **Column** check boxes associated with the **Inside Borders** option.

   This will apply a custom 2 pt. ruling to the outside edges of your selection, without affecting the interior boundaries in your selection. This might be useful for highlighting a specific row.

6. Click the **Apply** button.

7. Click anywhere outside of the cell to deselect it.

   The custom ruling of **2.0 point** is applied to the outside edges of the row, but not to the interior boundaries within the previous selection.

   If you followed these examples, your table should look something like the one shown here.

8. Select **File > Save**, and then **File > Close** from the main menu.

Table 3. **Advantages and Disadvantages of Cabling**

[]	[Advantages]	[Disadvantages]
[Co-axial cable]	• [[[Can run unboosted for longer distances than twisted-pair cable]] • [[Can transmit voice, video, and data]] • [[Technology used is standard]]]	• [[[Rigid cables may cause difficulty installing]] • [[More expensive than twisted-pair cable]]]
[Twisted-pair cable]	• [[[Low in cost]] • [[Easy to connect devices]]]	• [[[More prone to interference than coaxial or fiber-optic cable]] • [[Lower data transmission range]]]
[Fiber-optic cable]	[High-speed data transfer rates] [No magnetic or electrical signals, so no interference with sensitive external equipment]	[Difficult to install and connect devices to it] [High cost, both to purchase and install]

Chapter 12: Generating Books, Tables of Contents, and Indexes

Introduction

In this module, you will be introduced to FrameMaker's book management capabilities. You will learn how to create a book and generate a Table of Contents and an Index.

Module Objectives

In this module, you will learn how to:

- Generate a book.
- Add files to the book.
- Rearrange the book files.
- Generate and format a Table of Contents.
- Generate and format an Index.
- Update and validate the book.
- Set up page sides, and the page, paragraph, and chapter numbering of book files.
- Use the Element Catalog to insert Index marker elements.
- Edit existing index markers.

Creating A Book

A book is a FrameMaker file containing references to other FrameMaker document files.

 A book file is small in file size because it does not hold the chapters and graphics you might associate with a book or project. It simply keeps track of related files and manages their relationship to each other.

Use books to:

- Combine several documents (or chapters) as one larger document.
- Generate a Table of Contents, Index, List of Figures, or List of Tables for several files.
- Allow continuous page numbering across multiple chapters or files.
- Allow paragraph autonumbering to be continuous across multiple files.
- Allow updating of chapter numbering, paragraph numbering, page numbering, and cross-references across multiple files.
- Open, save, print, and close all files at once.
- Enforce consistent formatting by importing formats from one file to some or all of the files in the book.

 Saving a book file in the same directory as the files it references simplifies the display of path names within a book window.

Exercise 1:   Generating a book

In this exercise, you will create and save a book.

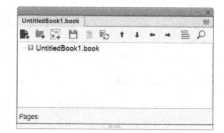

1. Select **File > New > Book** from the main menu.

   The book window displays on the left side of the document window, with the book file **UntitledBook#.book** automatically generated.

   Next, you will save the book with a descriptive name and appropriate location.

If you have any open content docs open, you will get a dialog box displays, asking **Do you want to add the file {filename}.fm" to the new book?**
Click the **No** button if you see this dialog. You'll add files in subsequent exercises.

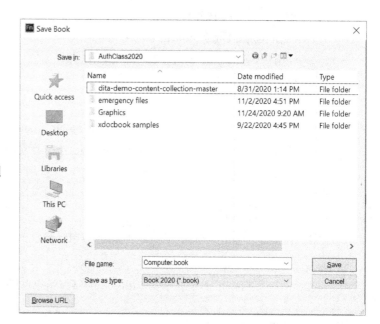

2. With the book selected as your active document, select **File > Save Book As** from the main menu.

   The **Save Book** dialog box displays.

3. In the **File name** text box, navigate to your `AuthClass2020` directory and save the book as `Computer.book`

   You can also use .bk as the file extension for a FrameMaker book file .

4. Click the **Save** button.

   Note that the book now displays its name and path.

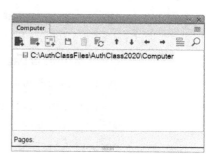

Exercise 2:   Adding files

In this exercise, you will add three more chapters to the book.

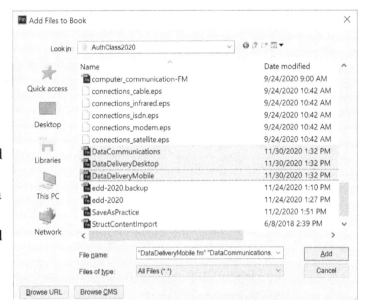

1. Click the **Add File** button () in your book window.

   The **Add Files to Book** dialog box displays.

2. In the file scroll list, select `DataCommunications.fm`, and then click the **Add** button.

   The `DataCommunications.fm` file is added to the book.

3. Use the **Add File** button ( ) to add the `DataDeliveryMobile.fm` and `DataDeliveryDesktop.fm` to your book file.

The book window displays the added files.

At this point, your Structure View contains a series of **BOOK-COMPONENT** elements. These will be recognized as **Chapter** elements when you update the book later in this chapter. You can choose to update the book now using the **Update Book** button ( ) in the book file panel, but if you do, some screen captures may differ slightly from what you see in the book.

4. Click the **Save Book** button ( ) in your book window.

✓ You can use the Shift and Control modifiers in Open, Save, and Add dialogs in FrameMaker.

Generating a Table of Contents

A table of contents can be generated for a single file or for a book. While you can generate a **Table of Contents** for a single file, in this section we'll focus on generating a TOC for our book file.

 ## Exercise 3:   Adding a table of contents

In this exercise, you will add a **Table of Contents** and an **Index** to the book.

1. From the book window, select the icon ( ) to the left side of the first file in the book.

2. Select **Insert > Create TOC** from the main menu.

The **Set Up Table of Contents** dialog box displays. Because you chose the location closest to where the TOC will go in the book, the **Add File** setting is showing an appropriate choice.

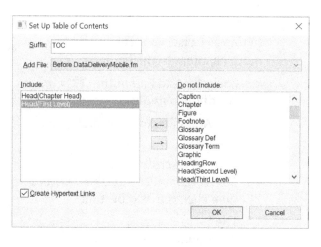

3. Move the following elements from the **Do not Include** scroll list to the **Include** scroll list:

- **Head (Chapter Head)**
- **Head (First Level)**

4. Select (turn on) the **Create Hypertext Links** check box.

   Hypertext links will be added to the **Table of Contents**.

5. Click the **OK** button.

   The **Update Book** dialog box displays.

6. Click the **Update** button.

   The **Update Book** function processes the files in the book and generates a list of the **Head(Chapter Head)** and **Head(First Level)** elements you specified for the TOC.

   The labels you chose are known as *context labels*, defined by your template and they allow you to differentiate between the various **Head** elements you have created throughout your document.

7. Open the `ComputerTOC.fm` document.

   The **Table of Contents** file opens. As you can see, the content exists, and there are page numbers showing the location of the sections within your document.

   However, the TOC has only default formatting.

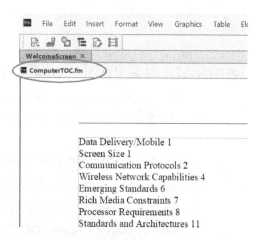

There is an interface bug that exists in FrameMaker up to and including version 16.0.1 that prevents the TOC from opening into its own pane the first time you open the file. As a result you'll see something like this the first (and only the first) time you open the TOC.

8. (If necessary) Select **Window>Consolidate** from the main menu to position the file with the other tabbed documents.

 If your TOC is the only panel open (other than the WelcomeScreen), then you may find Consolidate is unavailable. Other solutions to the floating window problem include dragging the title bar into the tabbed document area. You can also save, close, and reopen the file.

Formatting the table of contents

While you could format the TOC using the **Paragraph Designer** panel, if you are working in existing documents in a structured environment you will likely have a template available from which you can import formats into your "unformatted" TOC.

In order to import formats from a template, you'll need your template file open in FrameMaker.

 Exercise 4: Formatting a Table of Contents using a template

In this exercise, you'll import formats from a supplied TOC template file.

1. From the `AuthClass2020` directory, open the `toc.tpl.fm` file.

   The template file has no content, but contains the formats you need to add to your `ComputerTOC.fm` file.

2. Make `ComputerTOC.fm` the active document.

3. Choose **File>Import>Formats** from the main menu.

   The **Import Formats** dialog appears.

4. Set **Import from Document** to `toc.tpl.fm`.

5. Ensure that all options in the **Import and Update** section are selected.

6. Click the **Import** button.

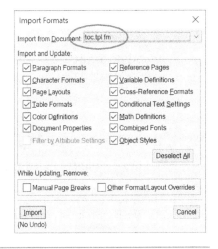

 Later in this chapter you will see that you can also import formats by selecting one or more files in your book file before using the File>Import>Formats command.

7. The formatting of the TOC improves greatly, but the page numbers are still not on the right margin with dot leaders. You'll fix that next.

Table of Contents

Data Delivery/Mobile 1

8. Select the **Update Book** button ()in the Book window.

   The Update Book dialog appears.

9. Select the **Update** button.

   If you get one or more **Inconsistent Numbering** messages, dismiss them. You'll set the file and page numbering in a future exercise.

   Your TOC now has the tabs and tab stop settings needed to complete the formatting.

Table of Contents

Chapter 1: Data Delivery/Mobile

 Importing formats brought in a different reference page definition for the TOC itself, which is why you needed to update the book, which in turn reprocessed the TOC.

Exercise 5: Adding an index

An index collects index markers into a generated list file in your book.

 The files that make up your book already have a number of index markers inserted; you'll learn how to add your own index markers later in this chapter.

1. From the book window, select the last file in your book.

2. Select **Insert > Standard Index** from the main menu.

    The **Set Up Standard Index** dialog box displays.

3. If not already selected, set *After DataDeliveryDesktop.fm*, in the **Add File** field.

4. If not already present, move **Index** from the **Do not Include** list to the **Include** list.

5. Select (turn on) the **Create Hypertext Links** check box.

    Hypertext links will be added to the index.

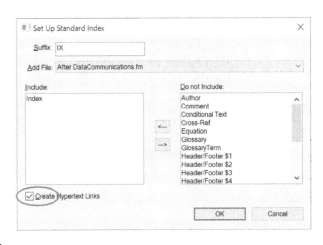

6. Click the **OK** button.

    The **Update Book** dialog box displays.

    Generated files need to be updated before you can use them.

    It is a good idea to leave all files in the **Generate** list so that they remain up to date, rather than moving specific files into and out of the **Don't Generate** list.

7. Click the **Update** button.

 As with the Table of Contents, if you get an Inconsistent Numbering Properties dialog, you'll need to accept the dialog to complete the update. This is a newly generated file, so its numbering properties do not yet match the rest of your book.

The `ComputerIX.fm` index file is now visible in the book file.

Notice that in the book window, generated files have colored icons. (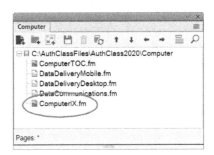)

8. Open `ComputerIX.fm`.

    As with the TOC file, when opening the index for the first time, the index will likely open into its own window, rather than into a tab with other currently open documents.

9. (If necessary) Select **Window>Consolidate** from the main menu to position the file with the other tabbed documents. As with the TOC, the IX will open into the tabbed interface after it has been opened the first time.

10. Select **File > Save** from the main menu.

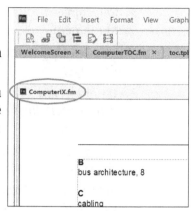

 If you skipped the Update process ( ) in earlier sections, you may see entries in the book file for the TOC and index, but they will not physically exist on disk until the book is updated.

Exercise 6:   Rearranging files in the book

You can reorder the files in a book by dragging the files in either the book window or the **Structure View**.

In this exercise, you will rearrange the files within the book window, putting the three chapter files in alphabetical order.

1. Click and drag `DataDeliveryDesktop.fm` to the position directly below `ComputerTOC.fm`.

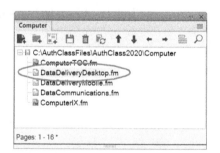

You haven't yet worked in the **Structure View** for the book file, but note that the corresponding elements in the **Structure View** for the book have also been reordered.

2. To finish the alpha sort, in the **Structure View**, drag `DataCommunications.fm` directly below `ComputerTOC.fm`.

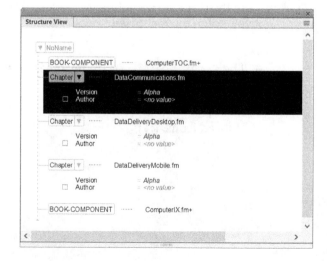

Formatting the index

Formatting an index is similar to formatting a **Table of Contents.**

 Exercise 7:   Formatting an index using a template

In this exercise, you will open an index template and import formats into your generated ComputerIX.fm file.

1. From the `AuthClass2020` directory, open your index template, `ix.tpl.fm`.

2. Ensure that `ComputerIX.fm` is your currently active document.

3. Select **File>Import>Formats** from the main menu.

    a. Set **Import from Document** to `ix.tpl.fm`.

    b. Select all options in **Import and Update.**

    c. Click the **Import** button

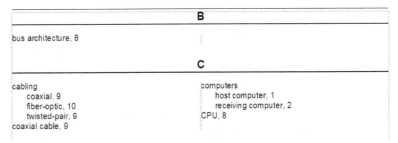

Your index file now has multiple columns, and the dividers now visually separate the groups from each other.

Index

B	
bus architecture, 8	

C	
cabling	computers
coaxial, 9	host computer, 1
fiber-optic, 10	receiving computer, 2
twisted-pair, 9	CPU, 8
coaxial cable, 9	

Updating a Book

You update a book (also refered to as *generate*) to:

- Update page sides, page numbering, and paragraph numbering.
- Update page sides, page numbering, and paragraph numbering, and chapter numbering, after editing files in book.
- Update text insets.
- Update cross-references.
- Populate **Table of Contents** or **Index** for the first time.
- Repopulate the **Table of Contents** or **Index**, after editing files in the book.

You have already updated your book in the process of generating TOC and index files. This section covers some of the other options we skipped earlier. You can speed up a number of tasks by performing actions to a series of files selected in your book. Numbering, pagination, import of formats, and turning on/off various indicators are all faster when performed across multiple files connected by a book file.

Exercise 8:   Turn off boundaries for your structured files.

Up to this point you've been working with visible element boundaries. Element boundaries do take up space and can slightly affect the page breaks and page numbering throughout the chapters, the TOC, and the index. For this reason, you'll start by turning off the boundaries in all files.

1. Open the `DataCommunications.fm` file.

2. (If necessary) Choose **View>Element Boundaries** to hide the element boundaries in the file.

3. Repeat steps 1 and 2 for `DataDeliveryDesktop.fm` and `DataDeliverymobile.fm`.

In FrameMaker 2020 you should find that the Element Boundaries (along with other things like Rulers, Borders, and Text Symbols) are application-wide settings, so you should only have to do this once, regardless of how many files are open.

Exercise 9:   Book update options

In this exercise, you will update your book file.

1. In your book window, select the **Update Book ( )** button.

   The **Update Book** dialog box displays.

2. If necessary, move `ComputerTOC.fm` and `ComputerIX.fm` into the **Generate** pane using the **Move Up** button.

3. Review the options for updating content in your book.

   The options above the **Generate** area help to ensure the content in your book is consistent and up to date.

   The **Apply Master Pages** option requires a master page mapping table on the reference pages of your documents. See *Assigning master pages to body pages* on page 219 of *FrameMaker - Working with Content* for more information.

4. Click the **Update** button.

5. Save all your open files.

Select the book file, press **Shift**, and select **File > Save All Files in Book** from the main menu.

Marking Text for an Index

Documents must contain index marker elements before anything will appear in a generated index. Different types of markers—**Index**, **Authors**, **Subjects**, **Markers**, and **References**— may be available in your content model, and used for generating different types of indexes. The **Insert Marker** dialog appears when inserting new **Index** marker elements.

You use the **Marker** panel, available at **Insert > Marker**, to edit existing index marker elements.

The table below shows several types of marker text entries and their appearance in the **Index**.

Document:	Marker Text:	Explanation:	Index Entry:
Tcalculator	calculator	single word	C calculator 2
TDog	dog	capitalization change	D dog 7
TAnn Smith	Smith, Ann	phrase, first name follows last	S Smith, Ann 3
TDog	Animals:Dog	single word, second level entry	A Animals Dog 9
Tcalculator	computer;calculator	single word, two entries	C calculator . . . . 3 computer 3
TDog	Animals:dog;dog	single word, second level entry; two entries	A Animals dog . . . . 9 D dog 9
Tcomputer parts and hardware	monitor, see hardware <$nopage>	no page number	M monitor, see hardware

Exercise 10: Inserting a basic index entry

In this exercise, you will insert a simple single index entry.

1. Navigate to the `DataCommunications.fm file`.

    If not visible, view the **Element Boundaries**.

2. In the "**Host Computer**"
    section, on page 1, place
    the insertion point before
    the phrase "**front-end
    processor**".

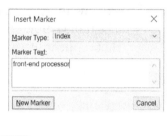

[[Host Computer] [This is the computer where centralized data is stored, where processing can be done, and from where information is transmitted. Mainframe host computers usually use a piece of hardware called a [**front-end processor**] to manage the Computer Communications of the network that the host computer is a part of.

3. Insert an **Index_Marker** element from the **Element Catalog**.

    The **Insert Marker** dialog box displays.

4. Enter `front-end processor` in the **Marker Text** field.

    This marker is a first-level Index entry. The phrase **front-end processor** will be alphabetically listed in the **F** section of the index.

5. Click the **New Marker** button.

    The **Index_Marker** element displays in the **Structure View**.

    Your actual index (`ComputerIX.fm`) doesn't yet contain your new index entry; you will update the index as part of a book update in a later exercise.

6. Select **File > Save** from the main menu.

 Exercise 11: Inserting second-level index entries

In this exercise, you will insert **Index** elements with slightly more complex marker text.

1. Still in the `DataCommunications.fm file,` locate the bulleted list, as shown.

    [[Principles of Computer Communications]

    [To understand Computer Communications, we will first look at some of the basic concepts involved. They are:]

    - [[[host computer]]
    - [[receiving computer]]

2. Place your cursor at the beginning of the `host computer` list item.

3. Insert an **Index_Marker** from the **Element Catalog**.

    The **Insert Marker** dialog appears, and displays **Index** as the
    Marker Type.

4. In the **Marker Text** text box, type:
    `computers : host computer`

    This marker text is a two-level index entry. In the index, under the **C**
    divider, the word **computers** will be listed as a first level index entry, with the phrase **host computer** listed as the (indented) second level entry.

An extra space before and after : and ; separators can help you read marker content and will not affect how the marker is processed or displayed.

5. Click the **New Marker** button.

   In the **Structure View**, the **Index_Marker** element displays.

6. Place the insertion point before the phrase "receiving computer".

7. From the **Element Catalog**, insert another **Index_Marker** element.

   The **Insert Marker** dialog displays.

8. In the **Marker Text** text box, type

   computers : receiving computer

   This marker text is another two-level index entry.
   Under the **C** divider, the word **computers** will be listed as a first level index entry, with the phrase **receiving computer** added to the existing **host computer** entry you placed previously, and listed as an indented second level entry.

9. Click the **New Marker** button.

   In the **Structure View**, the **Index_Marker** element displays.

 ## Exercise 12: Modifying existing index elements

In this exercise, you will locate and modify the markers of existing index entries.

1. In the **Structure View**, select the **Index_Marker** element bubble for host computer in the first bulleted item.

2. In the **Marker** panel, modify the **Marker Text** field to read:

   computers : host computer ; host computer

   The semicolon adds the phrase **host computer** to the index, as a separate entry in the **H** section.

3. Using this same technique, modify the entry for Receiving Computer by adding ; recieving computer to the end of the existing entry.

Reminder: An extra space before and after : and ; separators can help you read marker content and will not affect how the marker is processed or displayed.

4. Click the **Save** button to update your index marker.

 Your marker text will not be updated if you don't click **Save** in the **Marker** panel.

5. Select **File > Save** from the main menu.

Numbering and Pagination in a Book

You control the following numbering properties for each file in a book from the **Numbering Properties** dialog:

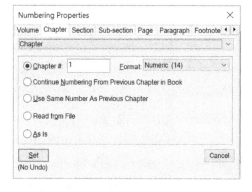

- Volume numbering
- Chapter numbering
- Section numbering
- Sub-Section numbering
- Page numbering
- Paragraph numbering
- Footnote numbering
- Table footnote numbering

Different files in the same book can have different numbering properties. The same options are available for non-generated and generated files.

First and last page options

For each file in the book, you can choose between single-sided and double-sided documents in the **Pagination** dialog. You can also choose the following options for double-sided documents:

- 1st page side
- Read from file (to use page side specified in the file)
- Next available page (used to avoid a blank page)
- Left or Right page

The **Pagination** dialog also dictates the behavior taken when you save or print documents.

The following are available in the **Pagination** dialog box, **Before Saving or Printing** options:

Choose:	To:
Read from File	Use file's current first page side, page side unchanged.
Next Available Side	Page side of first page based on page side of last page in previous file.
Left	Forces the first page to start on a left page
Right	Forces the first page to start on a right page.

Exercise 13: Setting up the book files

In this exercise, you will set up the page side, and the page, paragraph, and chapter numbering for each file in the book.

1. Select `ComputerTOC.fm` in the `Computer.book` file and select **Pagination** located in the **Format>Page Layout** menu item.

   The **Pagination** dialog displays.

2. If not selected already, select the **Double-Sided** option.

3. Ensure **Delete Empty Pages** is selected from the **Before Saving & Printing** field.

4. Click the **Set** button.

5. (Optional, if necessary) If an **Undo** alert displays, consider selecting the **Do not show again** option.
   Click on the **OK** button.

6. Right-click on the `ComputerTOC.fm` and select **Numbering** from the File menu.

   a. The **Numbering Properties** dialog displays.

   b. Select the **Page** tab.

   c. Ensure the **First Page** radio button is selected, and set the **First Page #** field to 1

   d. Set the **Format** field to **roman (xiv)**.

   e. Click the **Set** button.

   The first **Table of Contents** page number displays as roman numeral "i".

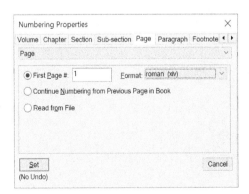

7. Right-click on the `DataCommunications.fm` file and select **Pagination** from the File menu.

    The **Pagination** dialog box displays.

    a. If not selected already, select (turn on) the **Double-Sided** radio button.

    b. Ensure **Delete Empty Pages** is selected from the **Before Saving & Printing** drop-down menu.

    c. Click the **Set** button.

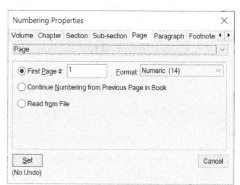

8. In the book window, right-click `DataCommunications.fm` and select **Numbering**.

    The **Numbering Properties** dialog box displays.

    a. Select the **Page** tab.

    b. If not selected already, select (turn on) the **First Page #** radio button, and in the text box type 1

    c. If not selected already, from the **Format** drop-down menu, select **numeric (14)**.

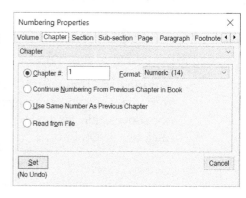

    d. Click the **Chapter** tab.

    e. Ensure that the **Chapter #** field is set to 1 and that the **Format** field is set to **Numeric (14)**.

    f. Click the **Set** button.

       This document is set up to use a **Chapter-Page** numbering scheme, as in *Page 1-1*.

       The initial "1" represents the chapter number, and the second "1" is the first page number.

You can perform many common tasks on multiple files using the book window. These include importing formats, and setting numbering and pagination options.

9. Select `DataDeliveryDesktop.fm`, `DataDeliveryMobile.fm`, and `ComputerIX.fm` in the book window.

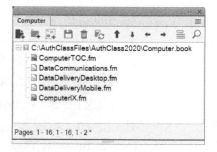

10. In the book window, right-click on your selection and select **Pagination** from the context menu.

    The **Pagination** dialog box displays.

    a. If not selected already, select the **Double-Sided** option.

    b. If not selected already, select **Delete Empty Pages** from the **Before Saving & Printing** menu.

    c. Click the **Set** button.

11. With the three files still selected in the book window, right-click the selection and choose **Numbering**.

    The **Numbering** dialog box displays.

    a. Select the **Page** tab.

    b. If not selected already, select (turn on) the **First Page #** radio button, and in the text box type 1.

    c. If not selected already, set the **Format** field to **numeric (14)**.

    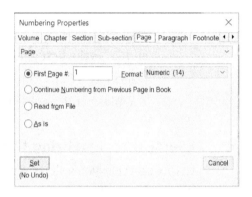

    d. Click the **Chapter** tab.

    e. Select the **Continue Numbering from Previous Chapter in Book** option.

    f. Click the **Set** button.

    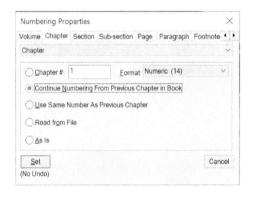

    The first page number in `DataDeliveryDesktop.fm` now starts with 2-1. The "2" represents the chapter number, and "1" is the first page number.

    g. Select **File > Save** from the main menu.

    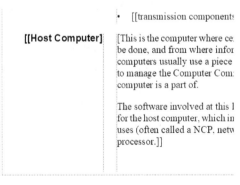

159

The index file will require special handling for the page numbering. In this final step, you'll create a custom label to replace the chapter number, which isn't applicable for the index.

12. Right-click on `ComputerIX.fm` in the book file, and select **Numbering**.

    The Numbering Properties dialog appears.

    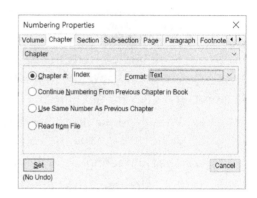

    a. Click the **Chapter** tab.

    b. Ensure the **Chapter #** radio button is selected.

    c. Type `Index` into the **Chapter #** field.

    d. Click the **Set** button.

       The first page number in the index now starts with "Index-1". "Index" represents the chapter, and "1" is the first page number.

    e. Select **File > Save** from the main menu.

       The files in the book are now set.

Exercise 14: Finalizing the book structure

In this exercise, you will correct errors in the book structure to create a valid book.

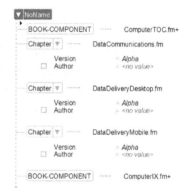

1. Observe the missing attribute values in the **Structure View** for the book.

If you try to edit the attributes at the book level, you'll get an error message.

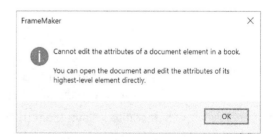

Because of this you'll need to edit the author value in each of the three individual chapter files.

2. Set the **Author** attribute value to your name in `DataCommunications.fm`, `DataDeliveryDesktop.fm`, and `DataDeliveryMobile.fm`.

3. Click the Update button (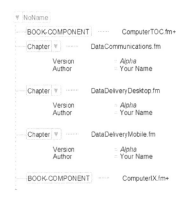) to update `Computer.book`.

   The revised attribute values now display in the **Structure View**.

4. In the **Structure View**, select the **NoName** element bubble.

   The container element for the book was created automatically, so FrameMaker doesn't quite know what it is, resulting in the **NoName** label.

5. With the **NoName** element selected, select **Book** from the **Element Catalog** and click the **Change** icon.

   The **NoName** element changes into a **Book** element.

   Finally, the two generated files are represented by unstructured documents, and have a BOOK-COMPONENT label.

   Because these files are unstructured, they need to be wrapped in an element from the **Element Catalog**.

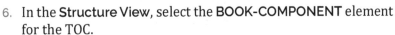

6. In the **Structure View**, select the **BOOK-COMPONENT** element for the TOC.

7. From the **Element Catalog**, select **TOC** and click the **Wrap** icon.

   The first **BOOK-COMPONENT** element is wrapped into the **TOC** element.

   Next, you'll repeat this process for the index book component.

8. In the **Structure View**, select the **BOOK-COMPONENT** element for the index.

9. From the **Element Catalog**, select IX and the click **Wrap** icon.

The second **BOOK-COMPONENT** element is wrapped with an IX element, but the red square indicates something is missing.

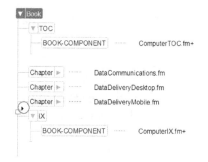

10. Position your cursor at the missing content, and note that the **Element Catalog** shows that **Glossary** is a valid element at this location.

   Rather than building a glossary using the **Element Catalog**, you'll need to add a glossary to the book file.

11. Click the **Add File** button () in your book window.

   The **Add Files to Book** dialog box displays.

12. In the file scroll list, select Glossary.fm, and then click the **Add** button.

   The Glossary.fm file is added to the book, but it is currently shown as a **BOOK-COMPONENT**.

⚠ Depending on your insertion point (or selection) in the book when you added the glossary, you may also need to move the inserted element to the position above the **IX**.

13. Update the book to get the file to recognize as a **Glossary** element.

   Your book now contains all the information necessary for a valid file.

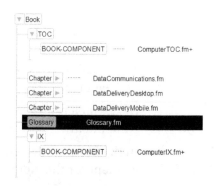

14. With the book window active (book selected), press **Shift** key, and then select **File > Save All Files in Book** from the main menu.

15. Select **File > Close All Files in Book** from the main menu.

Congratulations on completing your FrameMaker Structured Authoring workbook! You now have the skills necessary to create and edit content in a structured environment.

While your content model will differ from what you've used in this book, the concepts will remain the same. And just like in this book, in a very short time you'll know what the requirements of your new content model are, and how you can lean on your structured environment to efficiently do your job.

Need More FrameMaker Help?

Online courses available at courses.techcommtools.com

Experience a one-of-a-kind blend of live sessions, deep dive video sessions, and self-paced exercises without having to take 2 full days off of work.

Structured FrameMaker Interface

- Structured authoring (structured FrameMaker interface)
- Defining Element Definition Documents (structured FrameMaker interface)

Standard FrameMaker Interface

- FrameMaker - Working with Content (standard FrameMaker interface
- FrameMaker - Six-week online template workshop (standard FrameMaker interface)

Live training and development

Live online and in-person options are also available.

Spot training and problem solving

Book sessions as short as 1/2 hour at mattrsullivan.youcanbook.me

CPSIA information can be obtained
at www.ICGtesting.com
Printed in the USA
LVHW021055030221
678221LV00015B/718